C000175641

TRAVELLING
TO TRAGEDY

AN ANTHOLOGY OF GREAT TRANSPORT DISASTERS

DR RUDI NEWMAN

First published in Great Britain in 2017

Copyright © Dr Rudi Newman 2017

British Library Cataloguing-in-Publication Data
A CIP record for this title is available from the British Library

ISBN 978 0 85710 109 9

PiXZ Books
Halsgrove House, Ryelands Business Park,
Bagley Road, Wellington, Somerset TA21 9PZ
Tel: 01823 653777
Fax: 01823 216796
email: sales@halsgrove.com

An imprint of Halstar Ltd, part of the
Halsgrove group of companies
Information on all Halsgrove titles is
available at: www.halsgrove.com

Printed and bound in India by
Parksons Graphics

*To my parents and friends for their
encouragement, support and perseverance.*

Contents

The Author wishes to thank in particular the generosity of
David Lawrence, David Lean, Senan Molony,
Edward Petruskevich, Eric Sauder and Dan Smith in granting
access to their collections and expertise.

The Author

Dr Rudi Newman has a long-standing passion for all things historical, particularly in his specialist field of transportation. Having previously researched various maritime themes, his PhD centred on Victorian railways and their early impacts. A collector of transportation ephemera supporting his historical research, he has assisted with museums and exhibitions on a range of related subject matters and has presented numerous lectures and articles on transportation themes. Formerly the Honorary Secretary and Editor of the British Titanic Society, he has also acted as an advisor for several media interviews and documentaries.

Preface

Disasters have grabbed the human imagination since antiquity. Whether for heroism or arrogance, folly or fate, these tales show the best and worst of humanity when faced with extreme danger. The events chronicled here were of tremendous importance, yet while some have risen to legendary proportions – cloaked by myth and error – others have become all but forgotten in spite of their shocking details.

The origins of this book lie with an annual University history conference at which I was regularly invited to lecture. Gratifyingly, the presentations were very well received – many crediting them with being an eye-opener into new fields of study. The main reaction after this interest, though, was how little was really known of even the most famed of these incidents, while the majority have already slipped into relative obscurity. Calls to make the lectures more widely available, for this very reason, thus resulted in this book.

While by no mean exhaustive accounts, each chapter is intended to fulfil two aims: firstly, to introduce a new audience to both previously-unknown events and lesser-known information on famed disasters that have succumbed to inaccurate myths and legends. To this end, there is a short bibliography for anyone interested in learning more. Secondly, and conversely, each event in these pages is a detailed, self-contained and accurate summary based on the latest research, enabling a comprehensive understanding of what happened and why – but without assumptions, generalisations or fundamental omissions. Even for those who are familiar with these disasters, it is hoped all will find such updates of interest.

These disasters are, however, more than simply a collation of stories of tragedy. In the case of the Tay Bridge Disaster, it also presents new answers to a Victorian mystery – the cause of arguably the most infamous rail accident in history. But more importantly they are a warning to the future about what can happen if lessons are not learnt; the dangers of arrogance, inattention and carelessness amongst others.

Quoting philosopher George Santayana:

'Those who cannot remember the past are condemned to repeat it.'

THE BELLES OF BELFAST
The Olympic Class Liners

A century ago the world changed. It changed with news of a dark silhouette against the night sky; of howling screams, the icy cold, silence, and a lone voice whispering 'she's gone'. The maiden voyage of the world's largest ship had come to a disastrous end. Her name became infamous.

TITANIC

The ensuing disaster had such significance that a hundred years later virtually everyone knows of its details – it is part of our very culture. Books abound on the subject, but much of this is taken out of context or seen with hindsight, making logical and rational actions over a greater period seem strange or even lunatic. Myths and errors perpetuate, giving false 'truths' to a complex series of coincidences and mistakes. Now seen as almost legendary, many may think that the story took barely three hours to occur but actually it spanned more than three decades, and is yet to reach a final conclusion. Furthermore, *Titanic* was only one of three 'unsinkable' super-liners, her sisters being subject to calamity themselves. Fascinating in their own right, it is only by investigating all three

3722 A   WHITE STAR LINER "TITANIC."   ROTARY PHOTO, E.C.
LENGTH 882 FT. 6 INS.   BREADTH 92 FT. 6 INS.   45,000 TONS.

Period (pre-sinking) postcard of *Titanic* departing from Southampton. *Author's collection*

sisters and discovering their full story that we can properly understand the most famous of all maritime disasters. Dubbed 'Queens of the Ocean', this is the history of the Royal Mail steamships *Olympic*, *Titanic* and *Britannic*.

In 1845 Henry Wilson and John Pilkington began a joint partnership as shipbrokers chartering sailing vessels. Their company, the White Star Line, started purchasing their own vessels, however, expanded at a rate too fast for their budget and was declared bankrupt in 1869. For the sum of £1000 the company was purchased by Thomas Henry Ismay, backed by the company of a friend's nephew: Harland & Wolff shipyard of Belfast.

Registered as the Oceanic Steam Navigation Company, although still popularly known as the White Star, the company began commissioning steamships from Harland & Wolff till by the turn of the century it was one of the two largest British shipping firms, the other being the Cunard Steamship Company. In 1899 Thomas Ismay died, the business transferring to his son Joseph Bruce Ismay. By 1902 many shipping lines were in financial difficulties and financier John Pierpont Morgan (the inspiration behind the 'monopoly' man) began buying them out for his International Mercantile Marine Company, the IMM. Paying hugely over the odds at 32 million dollars (approximately ten million pounds), he acquired the highly successful White Star in 1902, with Ismay retaining the role of Managing Director. In 1904 Ismay accepted the position of President of the IMM.

However, events leading up to *Titanic* started in September 1907. For many years Cunard had been owners of the largest and fastest vessels afloat. Angry at having lost the coveted 'Blue Riband' speed trophy in 1897 to the German liner *Kaiser Wilhelm der Grosse*, which was also the largest ship afloat, they made an arrangement with the British Government to construct two new liners. The Admiralty was concerned at the American takeover of White Star, as it potentially prevented commandeering their ships in time of war. Therefore the new liners *Lusitania* and *Mauretania* were to become 'Armed Merchant Cruisers' if the need arose. With the September maiden voyage of *Lusitania* – now the world's largest and fastest liner – White Star was at a great disadvantage and threatened to lose its best clientele to Cunard along with a significant portion of the lucrative emigrant trade.

That year the Chairman of Harland & Wolff and former Mayor of Belfast, William Pirrie, invited Ismay and his wife to dinner at his Belgrave house. After dinner, discussion turned to *Lusitania* and *Mauretania* and the difficulties they posed to their companies. There was only one option: to build a new liner. Realistically they could not compete in terms of speed so they turned to size, luxury and safety. Furthermore, with a third Cunarder already being designed they would construct three new vessels of the same Class. The evening ended with preliminary sketches and, to emphasise their great scale, appropriate names were chosen from Greek mythology – arguably directly competing with

Cunard's use of Roman province names. All ending with White Star's traditional 'ic' suffix, from the Olympians came *Olympic*; the Titans, *Titanic* and the Gigantes (giants), *Gigantic*.

It soon became apparent that Harland & Wolff in its current state was not capable of constructing them: the proposed dimensions of the Class were substantially larger than their biggest slipway. Therefore, the yard immediately began a massive redevelopment project. Three slipways were demolished and rebuilt as two. Atop of this a massive construction scaffolding was assembled by the Arrol

Company. The 'Arrol Gantry' was 840 feet long, 270 feet wide and 228 feet tall – the largest structure in Belfast. In addition a new dry dock needed to be built – the largest in the world, capable of holding 23 million gallons of water. Belfast was not the only place to require construction work: Southampton and New York required new docks and piers for the liners to moor. With the necessary infrastructure completed, construction could begin in earnest.

Period postcard of the Arrol Gantry, Belfast. *Author's collection*

The Olympic Class design was one of both tradition and modernity. At 882 feet 9 inches long, with a beam (width) of 92.5 feet, they were almost 100 feet longer than their nearest competitors, and stood 175 feet tall from keel to funnels. Constructed from steel plates assembled with approximately three million rivets, they were to be powered by 29 boilers feeding two four-storey tall quadruple cylinder vertical reciprocating engines, venting into an ahead-only central turbine, collectively operating three propellers. Their steam engines and outer propellers still remain the largest of their type ever fitted to a ship, and overall were second only to Brunel's *Great Eastern*. Still visible on the wreck, *Titanic's* hull number – 401 – was marked on virtually every part fitted: one of many reasons to ignore the popular but erroneous conspiracy theory of *Olympic* and *Titanic* being 'switched' as part of an elaborate but illogical insurance scam (the vessels ultimately being under-insured). The Class only required three funnels, however it was decided to add a fourth (acting as a ventilator) to suggest they would be as powerful as other four-funnelers of the time. As a final example of scale were the sisters placed in Trafalgar Square, London, their funnels would just eclipse the height of Nelson's Column. No wonder they were considered almost 'monstrous'...

Comprising ten decks plus a double-bottom, they were divided from bow to stern with 15 transverse bulkheads ranging in height from C Deck to F Deck. The Class was designed so that any two adjoining compartments, or either the first four or last three compartments, could be flooded with no risk to the vessel – something unprecedented in ship design; one breached compartment usually

Period postcard comparing *Olympic* to the great buildings of the day. *Author's collection*

being sufficient to sink the average vessel. In addition they had the most powerful wireless sets of any vessel afloat, with a range of over 400 miles.

In terms of accommodation, they were subdivided into the three common classes of the day. Steerage (Third Class) was comparatively utilitarian, but still superior to many other vessels, and located toward the bow and stern. Second Class primarily occupied the area behind the fourth funnel and was considered better than First Class on many other ships. First Class was primarily located under the forward two funnels and had the greatest luxury. In addition to the ornate dining rooms, smoking rooms and lounge, the Olympic Class provided an à la carte restaurant, electric lifts, a squash court and a Turkish bath, and were among the first vessels to have a swimming pool and gymnasium. However, the focal point was the grand staircase, sporting a decorative clock entitled 'honour and glory crowning time'.

Designer Thomas Andrews. *S.F. Bullock, Thomas Andrews Shipbuilder; Project Gutenberg*

Olympic's keel was laid on No. 2 slip on 16th December 1908; *Titanic's* on No. 3 slip on 31st March 1909. Leading the design team were Alexander Carlisle and Thomas Andrews. Both leading naval architects, Andrews was also Pirrie's nephew. Constructed simul-taneously, White Star employed Harland & Wolff on a

9

The World's Greatest Gantry, in Harland and Wolff's North Shipyard, Belfast.

Period postcard depicting *Olympic* (right) and *Titanic* (left) under construction. *Author's collection*

cost-plus basis, utilising the best materials available, so later claims of being poorly designed and constructed are unfounded. There were occasional misfortunes – nine people were killed during *Olympic's* construction and eight with *Titanic's*. The Yard were surprised, as shipbuilding usually led to greater deaths than this – it often being claimed that for every £100,000 spent there would be a fatality. The cost of *Olympic* and *Titanic* was £1,500,000 each; approximately £85,590,000 today.

Period postcard of Olympic's launch. *Author's collection*

Olympic was launched on 20th October 1910 amid great publicity. Painted grey to aid Press photographers, her launch took the size record from *Mauretania* and as such there was major interest in the new liner. In 1911 The *Shipbuilder* journal published a special edition on the two new vessels, concentrating on their design and construction.

When referring to one of their safety features, the watertight doors, they stated:

'Each door is held in the open position by a suitable friction clutch, which can be instantly released by means of a powerful electro-magnet controlled from the

*captain's bridge, so that in the event of accident, or at any time when it may be considered advisable, the captain can, by simply moving an electric switch, instantly close the doors throughout and make the vessel **practically unsinkable**.'*

The Press subsequently dropped the 'practically', and so a legend was born – one that Harland & Wolff and White Star did little to counter; a proposed (but never released) brochure reading:

*'**As far as it is possible to do so**, these two wonderful vessels are designed to be unsinkable.'*

The Class's davits, specially designed by the Wellin Davit Company, could hold four lifeboats each, making a total of 64 boats. However, the legislation concerning lifeboat provision had only last been updated in 1894. It linked lifeboat numbers to overall tonnage; vessels over 10,000 tons to have 16 lifeboats. *Olympic* and *Titanic* were 45,000 tons each. Carlisle wanted 64 boats, but Ismay and Pirrie saw no need – particularly with a 'practically unsinkable' vessel. They also noted

Lifeboats and davits on the Boat Deck, *The Deathless Story of the Titanic*. © The British Library, 'Lloyd's Weekly News' 1912 special

that filling the decks with lifeboats would be unsightly and display a lack of confidence in their own vessels. On 30th June 1910 Carlisle retired (through ill-health), Andrews becoming Chief Designer. It was decided the sisters would have 16 lifeboats to comply with regulations and an additional four canvas-sided Engelhardt 'collapsible' lifeboats, totalling 20.

While *Olympic* was fitted out, construction continued on *Titanic* and she was launched on 31st May 1911. White Star never christened their vessels, so with little ceremony she slid into the Lagan; as one Harland & Wolff worker stated: 'we just build's 'em and shoves 'em in'. Once the 62 second launch was complete, signal rockets were fired spelling 'success'. None of the dignitaries knew that during the launch worker James Dobbin was struck by falling timber and died later that day; the eighth life lost constructing *Titanic*. *Olympic* was handed over to White Star the same day and proceeded to Liverpool, then to Southampton for her maiden voyage, commencing on 14th June 1911 to New

Captain Edward John Smith, *The Deathless Story of the Titanic*. © The British Library, 'Lloyd's Weekly News' 1912 special

3720 D   WHITE STAR R.M.S. "OLYMPIC,"
THE LARGEST STEAMER IN THE WORLD,
45,000 TONS, 882ft. LENGTH, 92ft. 6in. BREADTH.   ROTARY PHOTO, E.C.

Period postcard of the new *Olympic* in Liverpool. *Author's collection*

York. Her commander was Captain Edward John Smith, a man with forty-nine years at sea, and Commodore of the White Star. He was highly skilled and very popular – many millionaires changing their travel plans in order to sail with him. When once asked of his career, he replied:

'When anyone asks how I can best describe my experience in nearly forty years at sea, I merely say, uneventful. Of course there have been winter gales, and storms and fog the like, but in all my experience, I have never been in any accident of any sort worth speaking about… I never saw a wreck and never have been wrecked, nor was I ever in any predicament that threatened to end in disaster of any sort. You see, I am not very good material for a story.'

In 1907, on the arrival of the *Adriatic* after her maiden voyage under his command, Smith summarised his views on current maritime technology:

'I cannot imagine any condition which would cause a ship to founder. I cannot conceive of any vital disaster happening to this vessel. Modern ship building has gone beyond that.'

But things were about to change. On 20th September 1911, *Olympic* was en-route to Cherbourg and crossing the Solent with Smith and pilot George Bowyer on the bridge. Leaving the naval base, HMS *Hawke* drew alongside nearby. Suddenly she swerved into the aft starboard quarter of *Olympic*, puncturing her

Period postcard showing *Hawke's* crushed bow. *Author's collection*

hull and damaging a propeller. *Hawke* had her bow crushed, while *Olympic* limped to Southampton. She returned to Belfast for repairs with a wooden patch on her side and work on *Titanic* stopped. The inquiry blamed *Olympic*, as her engines literally sucked the smaller warship into her side. But White Star used the incident as a demonstration of how safe the Class was, as *Hawke* had a ram bow designed to sink vessels and had struck a bulkhead, thus flooding two compartments. In February 1912 *Olympic* threw a propeller blade and again returned to Belfast, work halting again on *Titanic*.

As with all new ships there were teething troubles: in *Olympic's* case primarily the underuse of the B Deck promenade. Modifications were thus made to *Titanic*: the primary two being that her B Deck promenade was replaced

Comparison of *Olympic* (left) and *Titanic* (right) showing the enclosed forward A Deck. *Author's collection*

with additional cabins, 'millionaires' parlour suites (with their own private promenades) and a café Parisien, while the forward A Deck promenade was glazed to replace the enclosed area lost on B Deck. Claims of this modification being due to spray appear to be unfounded. These changes collectively increased her tonnage, making *Titanic* the largest vessel afloat and giving her distinguishing marks from *Olympic*. Many of those who had previously sailed with *Olympic* would praise these modifications; third baker Reginald Burgess stating:

> *'Like the Olympic, yes, but much more elaborate. Take the dining saloon - the Olympic didn't even have a carpet, but the Titanic – ah, you sank in it up to your knees.'*

WHITE STAR LINE

THE LARGEST STEAMERS IN THE WORLD.

THE LARGEST STEAMERS IN THE WORLD.

"OLYMPIC" (TRIPLE-SCREW), 45,000 TONS,
AND
"TITANIC" (TRIPLE-SCREW) 45,000 TONS.

Period (pre-sinking) postcard advertising the two new liners. *Author's collection*

Olympic had received much publicity throughout her construction and early voyages, but it was *Titanic*, especially after these modifications, which had rising fame in the Press as a marvel of the age. However, in spite of the increasingly noticeable visual differences between the sisters, particularly the enclosed forward A Deck, due to their overall similarity many images of *Olympic* were – and still are – labelled as *Titanic*.

Due to the aforementioned delays *Titanic's* maiden voyage had been put back to 10th April 1912. Formerly under the temporary command of Captain Herbert Haddock, she was passed over to Captain Smith as he always took the maiden voyages of the company's new ships. On 2nd April she sailed into the Irish Sea for her trials, which due to bad weather delaying their start took less than twenty-four hours. All tests were passed and the Board of Trade certified her seaworthy. As she passed through Belfast Lough, a young boy called William MacQuitty watched from the shore. He had seen her launched in 1911, and considered her so enormous that she was:

> *'A toy ship sailing on a toy sea – she made the Lough look small.'*

Titanic arrived at Southampton just after midnight on 4th April, proceeding to load provisions and hire crewmembers. Owing to the delay in leaving Belfast she was not opened for public inspection, instead being dressed with flags. On 10th April Captain Smith re-joined the ship, having stayed in his Southampton home. It is believed that he intended to retire after the crossing. Previously Smith had ordered a reshuffle of officers, requesting Henry Wilde as Chief Officer from *Olympic*. As a result, intended Second Officer David Blair was taken off the crew and left behind. William

Cover of the company publicity brochure released to coincide with *Titanic's* launch. *Author's collection*

Murdoch became First Officer (instead of Chief), Charles Lightoller Second (instead of First), Herbert Pitman Third, Joseph Boxhall Fourth, Harold Lowe Fifth and James Moody Sixth. Hugh McElroy was the Purser and Joseph Bell Chief Engineer. Employed by the Marconi Company were wireless men Jack Phillips and Harold Bride, who were tasked with sending and receiving passenger telegrams. Also aboard were Ismay, who frequently sailed on maiden voyages, and Andrews with the 'guarantee group' from Harland & Wolff to ensure everything operated correctly.

Loaded aboard was a wide assortment of cargo ranging from mundane items such as mail, china and cotton to the unusual: cases of opium, a Renault, a vat of 'dragon's blood' tree resin and a Rubens painting. Most famous, however, would be a single book – a translation of the Rubaiyat of Omar Khayyam inlaid with 1,050 gold-set gemstones. But there was a lack of something more fundamental – coal. Shortly before she was set to

Period (pre-sinking) postcard promoting *Titanic* (actually a very heavily modified image of Cunard's *Lusitania* or *Mauretania*). *Author's collection*

depart, a miners strike led to a lack of coal for steamships, many being laid up in Southampton. This caused wide-scale unemployment in the town, enabling *Titanic* to effectively have the cream of Southampton's sailors. As *Titanic's* departure was to be headline news, and as it was estimated that she would use over 600 tons daily, coal was taken off other company ships to fill her bunkers – with one catching fire in the process...

At 8:00am on the 10th there was a brief boat drill for the crew and from 9:30am the special boat trains started arriving and passengers began to board. Tickets varied in price according to class and cabin location: the First Class 'millionaire's suites' cost £850 one way – approximately £48,501 today. The

Titanic in Southampton (a rare pre-sinking postcard genuinely depicting *Titanic*, dressed in flags on 4th April 1912). *Author's collection*

S.S. TITANIC.

cheapest First Class ticket was £26 – now £1483. Second Class was on average £13 – equivalent to £741 and Third Class ranged between three and nine pounds – today, up to £513. This was in a time when the average unskilled emigrant's wage was less than one pound a week; barely £57 today.

Boarding at Southampton were 922 passengers including William Stead the journalist; Major Archibald Butt, military aide to President Taft and Isidor and Ida Straus, owners of Macy's department store. Numbers were much less than anticipated for the crossing, possibly due to the temporary economic downturn caused by the miners' strike. Some passengers, mostly Second Class, were taken off other vessels stranded in Southampton, such as Eva Hart and her parents from SS *Philadelphia*. Some displayed concern lest anything would go wrong, but as a crewman said to Mrs Sylvia Caldwell: 'God himself could not sink this ship!'

At 12:00pm her mooring ropes were released and with the aid of tugs *Titanic* started her maiden voyage. Passing the line of moored ships, her propellers took the strain as Smith oversaw Pilot Bowyer (of the *Hawke* incident). Suddenly there was a crack, shouting and running about. The liner *New York* was moored nearby and the suction from *Titanic's* engines snapped her mooring lines like threads. As the vessel swung towards *Titanic's* stern, Smith set the port engine full astern – preventing a collision by mere yards. The tug *Vulcan* slipped off *Titanic* and took the *New York* out of the way as *Titanic* started again.

Her first port of call was Cherbourg, arriving at 6:30pm. She was too large to enter the port so moored at sea while 274 passengers, mail and cargo were transferred aboard by the tenders *Nomadic* and *Traffic*, with 22 disembarking. Of those taken by *Nomadic* – built specially to service the Olympic Class and now the last White Star vessel left – were Colonel John Jacob Astor IV, owner of the Waldorf-Astoria and his

Nomadic today on display in Belfast. David Lean

wife Madeleine; Benjamin Guggenheim the businessman; Margaret 'Molly' Brown the socialite and Sir Cosmo Duff Gordon, Fifth Baronet of Halkin and his wife Lucile, a famed fashion designer.

Her final stop before crossing the Atlantic was the port of Queenstown in Ireland, now called Cobh. Arriving at 11:30am on 11th April, again mooring out at sea, the last 123 passengers – mostly emigrants – and mail were brought aboard, with seven disembarking, making a complement of 1323 passengers and 885 crew; a total of 2208 on board. Departing from Queenstown *Titanic* headed for open sea, never to sight land again.

THE NEW WHITE STAR LINER "TITANIC." THE TWIN LARGEST VESSEL IN THE WORLD. 45,000 TONS GROSS REGISTER. 66,000 TONS DISPLACEMENT. LENGTH 882 FT. 9 IN. BREADTH 92 FT. 6 IN. ACCOMMODATION : 2,500 PASSENGERS, 860 CREW.

Period (pre-sinking) postcard of the new *Titanic* passing the Statue of Liberty (a heavily modified photograph of *Titanic* immediately after launch). *Author's collection*

From the 11th to the 13th *Titanic* covered 905 miles at almost top speed, sailing in fine weather. While the Marconi Company only had men on ships to deliver private messages, there was a common courtesy of passing ice warnings from ship to ship. At 10:30pm on the 13th the first message came in (by Morse lamp) of heavy pack ice from SS *Rappahannock*, which had sustained minor damage passing through it. *Titanic's* wireless broke down that evening. Phillips and Bride repaired it, against regulations, but had a large backlog of messages to send.

On Sunday 14th April *Titanic* received more warnings of ice ahead; the first from the *Caronia* at 9:00am. Divine service was held that morning concluding with the hymn *Eternal Father Strong To Save* – with the ironic line 'For those in peril on the sea'. Further warnings indicated much field ice and that it was more south than usual. One in particular from SS *Baltic* warned of ice 250 miles ahead of *Titanic*. Smith showed the message to Ismay who pocketed it – later showing it to some passengers while reassuring them that they would pass through the ice at full steam to avoid any danger. Eventually Smith asked for it back and it was posted in the Bridge several hours after being received.

Concerning Ismay's comments, many believe that he ordered Smith to increase speed or, according to Mrs Elizabeth Lines who claimed to have overheard them, strongly suggested that it would be an appropriate measure.

This is still strongly debated, but there are numerous points that nullify the argument. Firstly, Ismay as a passenger would have had no control over Smith as Captain while at sea. Secondly, a stoker stated at the Inquiry that boiler room one was not being used, therefore she could not have been going at the fastest possible speed – which might have damaged the new engines in any event. Thirdly there is the question of *why* go faster. Although earlier there had been impetus to empty the bunker in boiler room six that had been on fire, this was effectively put out by this point; although causing some warping of the bulkhead. There was no chance of breaking any speed records, it would be uneconomic with coal and had they arrived early Ellis Island immigration would have been closed – meaning everyone would have had to remain on board in any event. Arriving early at night would have also diminished

Period (pre-sinking) postcard of *Titanic* at sea.
Author's collection

the valuable publicity of completing the maiden voyage. Finally, they were sailing a slightly longer route as at 5:50pm Smith ordered a course correction to continue on a southern path, probably to avoid the reported pack ice. It should be noted that sailing at speed through ice was no unorthodox strategy – under the premise of being in the danger area as short a time as possible, increasing speed was common in this period.

With the temperature dropping, Lightoller relieved Wilde on the bridge at 6:00pm. At 7:30pm, three messages were intercepted from the *Californian* reporting large icebergs. Lightoller ordered the fresh-water tanks to be checked as it was nearing freezing by 8:40pm. Fifteen minutes later Smith excused himself from a dinner party and returned to the Bridge, discussing the weather and its impact on iceberg visibility. The evening was calm and clear; Lightoller later said it was 'like a mill pond'. This meant there would be no spray or breaking waves at an iceberg's base and with no moon there would be no reflection either. At 9:20pm Smith retired for the night, ordering to be woken 'if it becomes at all doubtful'. Shortly afterwards Lightoller sent word to the lookouts

First Officer William
Murdoch, *The Deathless
Story of the Titanic*.
© The British Library, 'Lloyd's
Weekly News' 1912 special.

to keep a sharp watch for ice. At 9:52pm the last complete ice warning was received, from the *Mesaba*. It was never delivered to the Bridge.

Lightoller was relieved by Murdoch at 10:00pm, while the lookouts were relieved by Frederick Fleet and Reginald Lee, who were told of Lightoller's earlier order to keep an eye out for ice. They had no binoculars; David Blair had unwittingly taken the key for the locker with him when disembarking in Southampton. It made little difference though – lookouts were trained to scan the horizon with the naked eye and only use binoculars for closer inspection, as elsewise they would be reducing their field of vision. By 10:55pm the Leyland Line ship *Californian*, also part of Morgan's IMM, found itself in the ice field between 10 and 19 miles north of *Titanic*. As it sent ice warnings to nearby ships the sensitivity of *Titanic's* set caused the *Californian's* message to override the private message Phillips was transmitting, and was so loud that it blasted in his ears. Crossly he replied 'Keep out! Shut up! You're jamming my signal. I'm working Cape Race.' Cyril Evans, *Californian's* Marconi man, was offended and at 11:35pm shut down for the night, his daily duties complete.

With First Officer Murdoch in command, Sixth Officer Moody assisting, Quartermaster Robert Hichens at the wheel and lookouts Fleet and Lee in the crow's nest, *Titanic* steamed forth at 22 knots. A slight haze had come into view on the horizon, possibly the distant ice field, visible for some ten minutes. The time was 11:40pm. Peering ahead, Fleet spotted a dark shape against the black sky – 500 yards and closing. He rang the ship's bell three times and picked up the phone to the bridge. Moody answered:

'What did you see?'
'Iceberg, right ahead!'
'Thank you.'

Murdoch shouted over to Hichens 'Hard a Starboard' and ran to the engine telegraphs, ordering all stop. He closed all watertight doors. *Titanic* gradually edged to port and slowed very slightly, but it was not enough. Broken ice from the berg fell onto the forward well deck, and as Murdoch ordered 'hard a port' to swing around the iceberg it drifted along the starboard side and out of sight. Barely a minute had elapsed since it was sighted.

Ever since, there have been arguments as to whether Murdoch did the right thing. Ordering full astern is a common myth; standard procedure was stopping, to limit cavitations and prevent any propeller damage. In any event, in the time before the collision the engineers could only attempt to slow down – there was no time to stop outright. Had there been binoculars Fleet might

A composite photograph and drawing of *Titanic* and the iceberg, *The Deathless Story of the Titanic*.
© *The British Library, 'Lloyd's Weekly News' 1912 special*

possibly have spotted it in time, though very unlikely, but some believe only a head-on collision would have prevented the sinking and human nature naturally tries to avoid such an action. Ironically, in 1903 Murdoch was praised for averting a collision on SS *Arabic* in this manner; disobeying orders and stopping a helmsman from turning the wheel. An experienced sailor, he plainly thought the iceberg was avoidable.

The force of the collision varied across the ship. Fleet and Lee were relieved about the 'near miss'. Boxhall was walking along the starboard A Deck and the

'Among the icebergs', a period postcard commemorating the disaster (based on the pre-sinking Statue of Liberty image). *Author's collection*

collision did not even interrupt his stride, despite the iceberg reaching up to the boat deck 60 feet above the water. Andrews was working in his cabin and failed to notice the collision. Some felt a gentle rumble, although most only realised something was afoot when the engines stopped. Mrs Ella White described the impact 'as though we went over about a thousand marbles'. In Third Class and the crew's quarters the ship shook and people were thrown out of bed. However, there was little concern. While stories of Astor saying 'I asked for ice, but this is ridiculous!' or of First Class passengers putting pieces of ice in their drinks are fiction, some Third Class passengers congregated on the Forward Well Deck and actually started playing football with broken pieces of ice.

Smith rushed to the bridge almost immediately after the collision:

'What did we hit?'

Murdoch explained. Calling for the watertight doors to be closed, he was told they already had been. Briefly ordering slow ahead, *Titanic* continued onwards for nine minutes before the engines were stopped permanently. Meanwhile he sent for Andrews and requested him, Boxhall and the carpenter to sound the ship for damage. They returned with bad news. The first six compartments were flooding, including boiler room six, and boiler room five was also taking a minor amount of water – collectively at a rate faster than the pumps could manage. Weighed down by the head, the bulkheads did not reach up to the watertight C Deck, allowing water to flow over their tops into undamaged compartments. In around two hours, *Titanic* would founder.

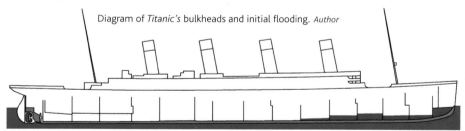

Diagram of *Titanic's* bulkheads and initial flooding. *Author*

Now one of the greatest misconceptions surrounding the disaster is actually what damage was done. Newspapers of the day reasoned that for an 'unsinkable' ship to sink in what appeared to be such little time, there had to be a tremendous amount of damage: a great gash in her side. But one man argued against popular opinion. Harland & Wolff architect Edward Wilding noticed that survivors' accounts of the flooding stated *different* levels in each compartment. He calculated that this was due to differing amounts of damage, as opposed to a continuous tear, and that the actual amount need not be particularly large – no more than 12 square feet. He put this forward at the Inquiry but was generally ignored. But in 1996 an expedition used sonar to locate the now-buried collision damage; a further expedition locating damage that according to Leading Fireman Fred Barrett literally opened up in front of him in boiler room six. Just above the silt, this small split, as with the others, was not a tearing gash but miniscule gaps between hull plates caused by the iceberg grinding along her side, buckling her plates and popping rivets.

The mythical 'gash' that sank *Titanic*; in reality a series of small gaps between hull plates. *J.B. Walker, An Unsinkable Titanic; Project Gutenberg*

There have been recent claims that she was sunk due to poor riveting – this was one of only two main areas aboard where they were fitted by hand instead of hydraulically. However, while a few rivets have shown high levels of sulphurous slag which at low temperature might have made it brittle, the majority of rivets were perfectly strong. As examples, at one point on the wreck there is now an 180° bend in the hull plating with no fracturing or failures. Although still debated, the sum total of the damage sustained is believed to be as follows: a trace amount in the forepeak tank, a 5 foot gap and a 4 foot gap in hold one, a 15 foot gap on the next bulkhead extending into hold two, a 32 foot gap across hold three and a 45 foot gap across boiler room six running into the bunker for boiler room five. The average height of each split is barely one inch. This tiny damage is hardly the 300 foot gash predicted – Wilding was right.

Titanic was now stationary but mortally wounded. Once called for, the officers immediately realised something was terribly wrong. Ismay noticed the collision and came to the Bridge, being informed of the situation. Lightoller was placed in charge of the port lifeboats, Murdoch the starboard boats, while the remainder were given various jobs; chiefly taking command of lifeboats. Shortly after 12:00am, 15th

Titanic's Boat Deck looking forwards, *The Deathless Story of the Titanic*. © *The British Library, 'Lloyd's Weekly News' 1912 special*

April, postal staff were seen trying to move mail to higher ground. Some purportedly became trapped and drowned; the first fatalities. By 12:12am the order to start bringing passengers on deck was given (initially First Class). Many First and Second Class passengers were unaware of what was happening, only that it had to be significant as the engines had stopped and the safety valves were lifting to reduce steam pressure, causing a tremendous noise. Third Class, however, had a better idea as water slowly inched up the walls of their cabins. But they had to remain below decks until the order was given to evacuate. Many of the officers realised that the lifeboats provided spaces for barely 1178 of the 2208 aboard.

Bride had just taken over from Phillips at 12:15am when Smith ordered them to prepare to send the international call for distress, CQD. Boxhall calculated their position, although in 1985 it was found this was out by 13.5 miles. At 12:25am the order was given to start filling the lifeboats: women and children first. Murdoch, to starboard, took this to mean that any remaining spaces were to be given to men. Lightoller, to port, assumed it meant women and children *only*. Although recognising the situation was serious, in a later interview he admitted at this time he still did not believe *Titanic* could sink. The ship's band, led by violinist Wallace Hartley, started to play rag-time in the First Class lounge, later moving up to the Boat Deck by the port entrance to the Grand Staircase.

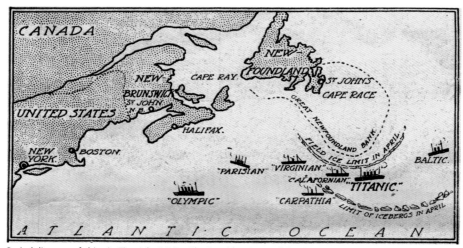

Period diagram of ships in *Titanic's* vicinity, *The Deathless Story of the Titanic*. © The British Library, 'Lloyd's Weekly News' 1912 special.

Smith returned to the Marconi room at 12:27am to tell them to start transmitting. Messaging until 2:12am, their calls were heard by numerous vessels – the *Mount Temple* (49 miles away), *Frankfurt* (153 miles), *Birma* (70 miles), *Baltic* (253 miles), *Virginian* (170 miles) and sadly also *Olympic*, some 500 miles away. They all had difficulty appreciating what was occurring; Captain Haddock, now commanding *Olympic*, repeatedly asking if *Titanic* was steaming towards them.

On the *Californian*, Second Officer Herbert Stone was watching the lights of a steamship that he and Captain Stanley Lord had sighted earlier. It looked as if she had also stopped, and they believed she was a similar-sized vessel to them – certainly not *Titanic*. They tried contacting it with a Morse lamp but received no reply.

At 12:35am Harold Cottam, the Marconi man on RMS *Carpathia* of the Cunard line, was undressing for bed having finished his shift, but happened to

Period postcard of the Cunard ship *Carpathia*. *Author's collection*

have his headphones still on. He was contacted by Cape Cod stating that there were messages queuing up for *Titanic*. Contacting her, he stated:

> *'I say, OM* [Old Man], *do you know there is a batch of messages coming through for you from MCC* [Cape Cod]*?'*

Philips simply replied:

> *'Come at once. We have struck a berg… …It's a CQD OM* [Old Man]*'*.

Cottam raced up to the bridge to inform the officer of the watch, then to the cabin of Captain Arthur Rostron. Rostron immediately ordered full steam to assist, ordering unnecessary systems such as heating shut down to conserve steam. Cottam informed Phillips that with a top speed of 14 knots they would traverse the 58 miles in four hours.

12:40am. Murdoch lowered the first lifeboat, No. Seven on the starboard side. Designed to accommodate 65, it left with 28 as many refused to board it. Not only was the drop from the boat deck to the sea so far that the water was barely visible, but many believed it far better to be on a large brightly-lit ship than in a small rowing boat in the Atlantic. Women refused to leave their husbands, and there was a comparatively relaxed attitude amongst passengers – after all, *Titanic* was 'unsinkable'.

Next launched was starboard No. Five, lowered by Lowe at 12:43am with 36 aboard, commanded by Pitman. Ismay tried to encourage women to board

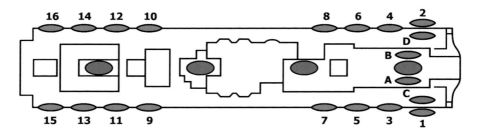

Diagram of *Titanic's* lifeboat arrangement (even numbers to port, odd numbers to starboard and collapsible boats lettered). *Author*

lifeboats, with one later saying that she owed her life to him. However, in his panicked attempt to assist with No. Five he repeatedly told Lowe to 'lower away'. Lowe lost patience and unwittingly told his employer: 'You want me to lower away quickly? You'll have me drown the whole lot of them!'

Around 12:47am Boxhall fired the first of eight distress rockets. He saw a vessel some miles away and attempted to contact it with Morse lamp, but it appeared to sail away. On the *Californian* Stone noticed the mystery ship was firing rockets. Unsure, he woke Captain Lord and described what he saw. Lord replied that they were probably company signal rockets, not all ships having a wireless set. Later Stone informed Lord that the unknown vessel appeared to have sailed away.

Lord's actions are probably the most contested aspect of the disaster. Ultimately blamed for not sailing to assist, Lord's reputation was ruined and his career effectively ended. However, since the discovery of the wreck it was found that Boxhall's position was slightly off. There is also argument about whether the correct type of rockets was used, as they were white instead of red. But the frequency of firing should have indicated distress – passenger Lawrence Beesley later stating: 'Anybody knows what rockets at sea mean'.

Still highly debated, many explanations have been offered such as optical illusions, conspiracy or simple misunderstanding. One popular suggestion is that a ship called the *Samson* that was illegally sealing was between the two vessels. This has, however, been conclusively disproved. While distances are sketchy, it seems most likely that the ships *Titanic* and *Californian* saw were indeed each other, but there will always be discussion over whether the ensuing inaction was understandable or culpable. In any event, Lord was to become an infamous scapegoat.

While Phillips sent distress calls, Bride took replies to Smith; at one point joking to Phillips:

'Send SOS – it's the new call. It may be your last chance to send it'.

Titanic firing rockets; *The Graphic* Saturday 20th April 1912. *Senan Molony collection*

They did not send history's first SOS; that title it is believed went to SS *Slavonia* in June 1909 after running aground off the Azores. Instead they interspersed SOS with CQD after 12:57am, using *Titanic's* call sign of MGY. The first SOS from *Titanic* was received by *Olympic*.

At 12:55am starboard lifeboat No. Three was launched with 32 aboard. As women were refusing to board, Murdoch allowed ten stokers in it. Port No. Eight left the ship shortly afterward at 1:00, with 39 people. Interestingly, considering the significance of class and gender in the era, the lifeboat was steered by the Countess of Rothes. Five minutes later, starboard No. One was lowered. Capable of holding 40 people, it carried only 12. Of these, seven were crewmen and five were First Class passengers, notably Sir Cosmo and Lady Duff-Gordon and their secretary. Becoming unpopular as a result, Sir Cosmo's action of giving each crewmember in that lifeboat five pounds to replace their lost kit worsened the situation, as it was seen by many as a bribe.

At 1:10am lifeboat No. Six on the port side was lowered by Lightoller with 28 aboard, including Molly Brown, Fleet and Hichens as tillerman. There was

Launching the lifeboats, *The Deathless Story of the Titanic*. © The British Library, 'Lloyd's Weekly News' 1912 special

also a solitary Third Class passenger – the first to depart. Partly lowered, they realised that the lifeboat was under-manned and called for assistance. Passenger Major Arthur Peuchen stepped forward explaining he was a yachtsman. Smith, who was nearby, suggested Peuchen descend to A Deck, break a window and climb in. But Lightoller told him that if he was a good enough sailor to climb down the rope falls to the lifeboat, only then could he crew it. As Peuchen jumped out and climbed down his wallet fell out of his pocket, but he made it into the boat. Later Smith would call them back as they were half-empty, but Hichens refused to turn around.

Around this time some passengers began noticing a slight incline to the previously level deck. Down below, Barrett and the stokers were busy manning the pumps and drawing the fires to prevent any boiler explosions, but there was little they could do other than continue trying to generate power for the lights and wireless. Some have claimed that the fire-damaged bulkhead separating boiler rooms five and six would have been unable to cope with the pressure of over seven *tonnes* of water entering the hull per *second*. Realistically it would have made little substantial difference; boiler room five was flooding in any event. At this point the crew was forced to run for their lives to the next compartment.

By 1:17am the mood began to change. There was now a noticeable list to starboard and the name on *Titanic's* bow was nearing the water – the decks becoming ever steeper. More people started to board the 14 remaining lifeboats. While most stories of Third Class being actively held back are myth, no-one appears to have remembered to send specific orders to *allow* them up. It was only by this point that Third Class passengers were coming up to the Boat Deck, having found alternative means of access on their own.

While this was occurring, port No. Sixteen was swung out at 1:20am with over 50 aboard, including the first substantial number of Third Class passengers. Five minutes later there were signs of panic amongst some of the passengers; several were about to jump into the full and half-lowered port No. Fourteen but Lowe fired shots into the air to warn them off.

Titanic was now listing to port as port No. Twelve was lowered at 1:30am with 40 occupants, starboard No. Nine being lowered simultaneously with 56 aboard. Starboard No. Eleven followed at 1:35am with 70 aboard – actually overloaded. This included Nanny Alice Cleaver, who is now frequently confused with a period child murderer of the same name. Phillips' messages started becoming more desperate; telling *Olympic*:

'We are putting passengers off in small boats.' 'Women and Children in boats, can not last much longer.'

1:40am. Starboard Nos. Thirteen and Fifteen were launched almost simultaneously, with 64 and 65 aboard respectively. While earlier lifeboats had been sent away part empty as the officers incorrectly feared that the davits could not hold the weight of a full boat, they now had to deal with an increasing surge of passengers; No. Fifteen being fully loaded. As it neared the water, No. Thirteen drifted under it, still attached to the falls. Barrett, commanding No. Thirteen, called up to stop lowering but was not heard. A passenger managed to cut them free moments before No. Fifteen would have crushed them.

At 1:57am *Carpathia* received their last message from *Titanic*, although other ships were still picking up transmissions. Port No. Two was lowered with 25 people under the command of Boxhall; the final rockets being fired only minutes later. 1:50am saw the launch of Port No. Ten with 35 aboard. These included the Dean family, who were emigrating to Kansas. Nine week old Millvina was *Titanic's* youngest passenger and would become the last survivor of the disaster.

Lifeboats rowing from the ship; Dutch artist Jan Lutz. *Senan Molony collection*

At 1:55am J.J. Astor asked Lightoller if he could join his pregnant wife in port No. Four. Lightoller refused, and the boat left with 32 people. It should be noted that while allowing fewer people to board than Murdoch, Lightoller was actually slower in launching his boats.

With most of the lifeboats gone, people started to move towards the

Last survivor Millvina Dean with the Author at the 2009 British Titanic Society Convention. *Author*

higher stern. As the Forward Well Deck began to submerge, her propellers rose out of the water, while those watching from the lifeboats could discern the dim lights of portholes slowly disappearing under the sea. At 2:00am Collapsible Boat C was about to be lowered when a 47th occupant boarded. Bruce Ismay.

Destroying his reputation, Ismay left *Titanic* in unknown circumstances. Coming close to a breakdown and later requiring sedation, he could not remember how he departed other than that the area around the collapsible was devoid of female passengers. Films popularly portray him as sneaking into the boat or even striding in as the owner, but some witnesses claim to have seen an officer, possibly Wilde, literally 'bundle' him in. American newspapers at the time were anti upper-class Englishmen, with many owned by newspaper tycoon William Randolf Hearst who had a long-standing personal grudge against Ismay. The newspapers thus painted a black picture of him – nicknaming him J. 'Brute' Ismay. To quote part of a period poem:

'The captain stood where a captain should,
For the law of the sea is grim,
The owner romped ere his ship was swamped,
And no law bothered him.'

Joseph Bruce Ismay, *The Deathless Story of the Titanic.* © The British Library, 'Lloyd's Weekly News' 1912 special

Ismay was only a *passenger* on board, and was deeply disturbed by the events unfurling around him – so much so that he could not bear to turn and see his ship sink. Senator William Smith, who would lead the American Inquiry, served papers to prevent Ismay leaving America until an Inquiry was held, but ultimately declared him innocent of any wrongdoing. Lord Mersey, head of the British Inquiry, equally concluded that:

'Had he not jumped in he would merely have added one more life, namely, his own, to the number of those lost.'

Nonetheless, the Press' negative viewpoint is what the public remembered, so Ismay effectively became another scapegoat; an unkind epitaph for a man who tried to save lives.

With only three collapsible lifeboats left, each capable of holding only 47 people, the officers feared a rush. Lightoller made crewmembers form a circle around Collapsible D, allowing only women and children through. Lowered at 2:05am with 24 aboard, he had to fire his revolver in the air to warn people off. With water less than 10 feet from A Deck, her foc'sle deck went under. Around this time the band stopped playing ragtime music. Hartley, a devout Methodist, had always loved a particular hymn and he and the band played *Nearer my God to Thee*. While some debate whether it was played, sufficient survivors recall hearing it, although nearly all the films have the wrong tune. Current research suggests that played was 'Propior Deo' by Sir Arthur Sullivan – the melody popularly used by Methodists, including Hartley's own father.

At 1:57am Captain Smith entered the Marconi room, relieving Phillips and Bride of their duties, but they continued calling for assistance. A stoker crept into the room and tried to steal Phillips' life jacket, but Bride fought him off as Phillips continued working. SS *Virginian* heard two faint 'V's from *Titanic* – a test signal while Bride attempted to counter the dwindling electrical output – and at 2:12am they heard CQ–, and it cut off: the final transmission from *Titanic*. With water flowing into the Bridge they left the room, Phillips heading aft and Bride arriving at Collapsible B just after it was moved from the port officers' quarter's roof – landing upside-down on the boat deck.

Captain Smith called out 'every man for himself' and according to legend the words 'Be British!'. He was last seen by Bride entering the water. According to one account, Thomas Andrews was seen alone in the First Class smoking room staring at a painting of the approach to Plymouth harbour as his creation sank beneath him, but he was later seen one final time near the Bridge with Smith. Murdoch was portrayed in the 1997 blockbuster film as shooting steerage passengers then committing suicide. He did neither – instead vainly trying to wind in the forward davits in order to lower Collapsible A until water came up to his knees. At 2:15am she made a sudden plunge, submerging the Bridge and causing Collapsible B to float free, still upside-down. Collapsible A also floated free but was swamped and in

The dashed dream: a period postcard depiction of *Titanic* (actually *Olympic*) underway.
Author's collection

Period postcard commemorating *Titanic's* band, with the Horbury version of *Nearer my God to Thee*.
Author's collection

'...Every light was blazing...'; *The Sphere*, 20th April 1912. *Senan Molony collection*

danger of sinking – its 20 occupants standing in icy water. At such an angle as to make the bulkheads useless, *Titanic* started her death throes. Lightoller jumped into the water, which 'was like a thousand knives being driven into one's body'.

He continues:

> *'The terrific strain of bringing the after-end of that huge hull clear out of the water, caused the expansion joint abaft Number One funnel to open up… The fact that the two wire stays to this funnel, on the after-part, led over and abaft the expansion joint, threw on them an extraordinary strain, eventually carrying away the port wire guy, to be followed almost immediately by the starboard one. Instantly the port one parted, the funnel began to fall, but the fact that the starboard one held a moment or two longer, gave this huge structure a pull over to that side of the ship, causing it to fall, with its scores of tons, right amongst the struggling mass of humanity already in the water. It struck the water between the Engelhardt and the ship, actually missing me by inches.'*

At 2:17am *Titanic's* stern cleared the water and all aboard scrambled for her aftermost deck. Her lights flashed once then were extinguished, leaving a black silhouette against the night sky. A rumbling crash echoed around – many believed it to be her boilers breaking free, but in reality her back was broken. Contrary to films and artwork she did not attain a now-stereotypical steep angle, now believed to be no more than 30°, and most did not notice her break up. In the process the hull area under the third funnel was torn into large chunks of debris and her great engines broke apart.

Settling slightly, the stern flooded almost instantly and reared up vertically, rotating 180°. Then at 2:20am, 15th April, 'like an elevator' she glided beneath the waves. A voice called out:

    'She's gone'.

Her last moments (in actuality she never attained such a degree before breaking up). *F. Young, Titanic; Project Gutenberg*

Those in the lifeboats could hear the screams of those in the water and many considered going back. However, only Lowe in No. Fourteen returned to help, rescuing four, one of whom died. Under Lowe's orders, boats Four, Ten, Twelve, Fourteen and Collapsible D were lashed together and passengers moved about to improve stability. Seven swimmers made it to No. Four, but two would die. Seven-year-old Eva Hart was with her Mother in lifeboat Fourteen. Originally booked to sail with the *Philadelphia*, they should not have even been there. Her father was still on board when *Titanic* disappeared. According to Eva:

'The sounds of people drowning are something that I can not describe to you, and neither can anyone else. It's the most dreadful sound and there is a terrible silence that follows it.'

Lifeboats 14 (right) and collapsible D (left), *The Deathless Story of the Titanic*. © *The British Library, 'Lloyd's Weekly News' 1912 special*

Molly Brown in No. Six would gain worldwide fame and the nickname of 'unsink-able', losing patience with Hichens – threatening to throw him overboard – and encouraging the female occupants to help row. Collapsible B remained afloat with 30 people standing on its upturned hull, including Lightoller and Bride. Lowe picked up survivors, but up to half were already dead. Survivors in Collapsible A were also picked up, with three further fatalities.

Lifeboat Six, *The Deathless Story of the Titanic.* © *The British Library, 'Lloyd's Weekly News' 1912 special*

An 'In Memoriam' postcard depicting Captain Smith and Jack Philips. *Author's collection*

At 4:10am *Carpathia* came into view, having sailed to them at 17 knots – three knots more than her design speed. Leaving the area at 8:50am for New York, Bride assisted Cottam with sending out messages informing survivor's loved ones of their rescue, even though he was suffering from severe frostbite. On board were 712 survivors. 1496 were lost. Among them were Captain Smith, Chief Officer Wilde, First Officer Murdoch, Sixth Officer Moody, Purser McElroy, Chief Engineer Bell, Jack Phillips, Thomas Andrews, Wallace Hartley and his band, William Stead, Major Archibald Butt, Isidor and Ida Straus (who chose to remain together), J.J. Astor and Benjamin Guggenheim – probably most famous for his last words:

'We are dressed in our best and are prepared to go down as gentlemen.'

It has since been calculated that the lifeboats had potentially up to 560 empty spaces.

Newspapers received scant pieces of information and released terribly inaccurate headlines, claiming *Titanic* was under tow and all were safe, until the *New York Times* made an educated guess and one of the greatest scoops in journalism history. White Star officials in New York originally contested any serious incident, highlighting *Titanic's* 'unsinkability', until a telegram from Ismay simply stated:

'Deeply regret advise you Titanic sank this morning after collision with iceberg, resulting in serious loss of life. Full particulars later.'

On 17th April White Star hired the cable-layer *Mackay-Bennett* to recover bodies, later also the *Minia*, *Montmagny* and *Algerine*. Next day *Carpathia* arrived in New York. She lowered the few recovered *Titanic* lifeboats in the White Star berth before proceeding to Cunard pier 54 to offload survivors.

The disaster was one of the first international media sensations – one of the reasons for its fame now. There was overwhelming grief and a demand to know what caused the sinking and such poor provision of lifeboats. Newspapers and periodicals devoted whole issues to the disaster and numerous books and pamphlets were rapidly published. A short story published in 1894 unexpectedly rose to become a best-seller. Entitled *Futlity*, it had previously been a flop; people considering it to be too fantastical. It told of a sailor on a fictional vessel – the largest in the world at some 800 feet long. Proclaimed unsinkable, the fictional Victorian liner had insufficient lifeboats when it struck an iceberg and foundered with the loss of most of those on board. The fictional ship was called the *Titan*.

The 'Titanic Disaster Relief Fund' was established in the immediate aftermath to aid those who had lost everything, with almost every town having special events to raise funds. The relief provided was necessary. To give an example, the male population of Southampton was decimated – almost every person knew someone who was lost. In one school alone, over 120 children lost their fathers. Small wonder why Southampton has the greatest number of *Titanic* memorials. Wallace Hartley was deemed a hero; for his funeral his home town's population *tripled*, with over 40,000 people coming to pay their respects. The other great popular hero was Jack Phillips, whose body was never recovered.

Reading the list of the saved, Southampton, *The Deathless Story of the Titanic*. © *The British Library, 'Lloyd's Weekly News' 1912 special*

Two Inquiries were held into the disaster: an American Senate Inquiry and a separate Inquiry by the British Board of Trade. The former lasted from 19th April to 25th May, chaired by Senator William Smith. The British Inquiry waited until the American was virtually concluded, lasting from 2nd May to 3rd July. Chaired by Wreck Commissioner Lord Mersey, it is now considered a whitewash as it was the Board of Trade whose regulations had led to the lifeboat situation in the first place.

The Inquiries mostly concentrated on how events unfurled, bringing in both experts and survivors to explain – most frequently, Ismay. Much discussion was made on the actions of the *Californian* and lifeboat numbers, resulting in one of the most bizarre of quotes. Harold Sanderson, vice-president of the IMM, stated at the British Inquiry:

*'I still do **not** feel it would be a wise or necessary provision to provide boats for everybody on board ship.'*

He was ignored and regulations modified so that all ships would have sufficient lifeboats for everyone aboard. Also twenty-four-hour wireless operation was made compulsory and the International Ice Patrol was founded in 1913 to chart the position of icebergs and warn vessels. Finally, the first 'International Convention for the Safety of Life at Sea' was held as a result in 1914, making many of these recommendations international law. 'SOLAS', as it is called, is still in use as the premier treaty on safety regulations at sea.

Only one vessel, the *Hans Hedtoft* of 1959, has foundered with loss of life through iceberg collision since. Coincidentally, she too was on her maiden voyage – and was considered by some to be 'unsinkable'...

The Inquiries, however, did make errors such as the iceberg damage and an incorrect timeline of lifeboat launches; much modern research being undertaken to correct their mistakes. Arguably the largest single mistake though was the manner of the final plunge. Most witnesses called were First Class, notably Colonel Archibald Gracie IV. Recognized as virtually the last person to leave the ship and survive, swimming to Collapsible B, he was adamant that *Titanic* sank in one piece. Several Third Class survivors conversely claimed to have seen her break up, but they were not called as witnesses.

Ultimately concluding 'The ship did not break in two' perhaps, still reeling for the sheer inaccuracy of *Titanic's* 'unsinkability', it was just thought unthinkable that such a strong vessel could have been torn apart; a similar mind-set to how the iceberg damage became characterised as the infamous fictional large 'gash'. In any event, this was to colour public perceptions of the final moments for over seventy years.

Lastly, the Inquiries estimated the total loss. Subdivided by class, the official figures reveal the difference in survival:

		SAVED	LOST	PERCENT SAVED
FIRST CLASS	WOMEN	140	4	97.22
	MEN	57	118	32.57
	CHILDREN	6	0	100
SECOND CLASS	WOMEN	80	13	86.02
	MEN	14	154	8.33
	CHILDREN	24	0	100
THIRD CLASS	WOMEN	76	89	46.06
	MEN	75	387	16.23
	CHILDREN	27	52	34.18
CREW	WOMEN	20	3	86.96
	MEN	192	693	21.69

Recent research contradicts the exactness of their figures, but it appears in total 712 survived and 1496 were lost. Of particular note are the engineers, none of whom survived, and two year old Loraine Allison – the only child lost in First Class (demonstrating the errors in the official table). Only 337 bodies were recovered, most being buried in Halifax, Nova Scotia.

While the Inquiries were progressing, White Star had two large problems – *Olympic* and *Gigantic*, whose keel was laid on 30th November 1911. *Olympic* had already had one voyage cancelled due to a mass stoker's mutiny: many refused to sail on a ship with insufficient lifeboats, so were replaced with non-Union stokers.

Period postcard of *Britannic* on the stocks.
Author's collection

Period postcard of Britannic in White Star livery (the image actually of *Olympic*). *Author's collection*

In protest at this act, the rest went on strike! It was decided to modify the sisters, rectifying all issues raised in the Inquiries – particularly lifeboats and bulkheads. *Gigantic* was renamed *Britannic* and had further modifications – additional stern decks and large gantry davits capable of lowering multiple lifeboats simultaneously. Launched on 26th February 1914, White Star claimed her:

'*As perfect a specimen of man's creative power as is possible to conceive*'.

Plainly it was hoped that she could rectify the bad publicity of *Titanic*. But it was not to be.

The Great War was a disaster far outweighing anything previously, with *Lusitania*, *Californian* and *Carpathia* all ultimately being victims. At its start the two sisters were called up. *Olympic* became a troop transport while the still incomplete *Britannic* became a hospital ship under the command of Captain Charles Bartlett. Both saw active service: *Olympic* rescued the crew of HMS

A period postcard showing *Britannic* off Mudros, Greece. *Author's collection*

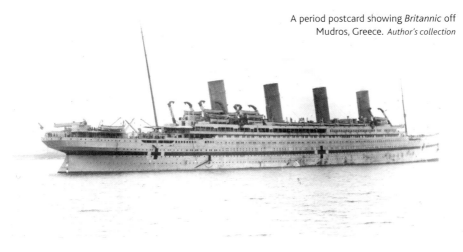

Britannic menu, 26th September 1916. *John Creamer collection*

Audacious after striking a mine and became the only merchantman in the War to sink an armed enemy when she ran over U-boat *U-103*. Meanwhile *Britannic* assisted at Gallipoli with five successful voyages repatriating wounded soldiers.

On 12th November 1916 His Majesty's Hospital Ship *Britannic* departed Southampton on her sixth voyage, bound for the island of Lemnos in the Aegean Sea with 1066 crew and nursing personnel aboard. Arriving at Naples for re-fuelling on the 17th, then briefly delayed in port due to a storm, she entered the Kea channel early Tuesday, 21st November.

At 8:12am there was an explosion. To quote nurse Violet Jessop:

'Suddenly, there was a dull deafening roar. Britannic gave a shiver, a long drawn out shudder from stem to stern, shaking the crockery on the tables, breaking things till it subsided as she slowly continued on her way. We all knew she had been struck...'

It was thought at the time to be either a torpedo or a mine, and has now been confirmed as a mine laid by *U-73* and Kapitänleutnant Gustav Siess; the mine securing anchors still littering the seabed. As everyone reported to their lifeboat stations, the full extent of the damage was identified. The hull was ruptured between holds two and three on the starboard side, however, the force of the explosion damaged bulkheads and jammed several watertight doors causing flooding in all of the first six compartments. Post-*Titanic* this was the new

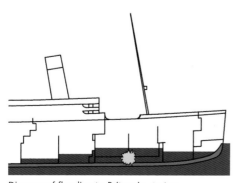

Diagram of flooding to *Britannic*. *Author*

maximum that she could sustain and survive. But many portholes had been opened by nurses who found their Atlantic cabins too stuffy for the Mediterranean climate. Her forward momentum forced water in, and as she listed more open portholes submerged – it was quickly realised that she would founder. Through this action, all of her safety devices were nullified.

As *Britannic* was sinking rapidly Bartlett decided to try and beach her on the nearby island of Kea, so ordered full ahead and attempted to turn her while transmitting distress signals. Simultaneously, officers and crew began preparing the lifeboats, awaiting the order to lower them. Amid the panic some had already been half-lowered. After a few minutes the order to wait was given. However, two lifeboats were launched without the knowledge of the officer in control, Third Officer Francis Laws. Violet Jessop was in one when it fell 6 feet into the water, and was surprised to find herself almost alone in it:

Period postcard of HMHS *Britannic* at sea.
Author's collection

'...*every man jack in the group of surrounding boats took a flying leap into the sea. They came thudding from behind and all around me, taking to the water like a vast army of rats. I turned around to see the reason for this exodus and, to my horror, saw Britannic's huge propellers churning and mincing up everything near them – men, boats and everything were just one ghastly whirl.*'

Jessop passed through the spinning blades as the lifeboat was torn apart. She survived with a fractured skull and cut leg. Amazingly, she had been a stewardess on *Olympic* when she struck HMS *Hawke*, and had survived *Titanic's* sinking too. Thirty other occupants of the lifeboats were not as fortunate.

Bartlett realised that she was shipping more water so ordered all stop – the propellers stopping just in time to prevent a third lifeboat from being drawn in. At 8:35am he ordered the lifeboats lowered and for everyone to abandon ship. Around 8.45 the engines were briefly restarted and evacuation paused; a second short-lived beaching attempt. But it was no good. With the Bridge about to submerge by 9:00am, Bartlett stepped into the sea after signalling for the engineers to evacuate. Due to the list, of 55 lifeboats only 35 were launced. At 09:07am she rolled over to starboard and foundered; Jessop recalling:

'*She dipped her head a little, then a little lower and still lower. All the deck machinery fell into the sea like a child's toys. Then she took a fearful plunge, her stern rearing hundreds of feet into the air until with a final roar, she disappeared into the depths, the noise of her going resounding though the water with undreamt-of violence...*'

Britannic took only fifty-five minutes to go down. 1036 survivors, including Captain Bartlett, were rescued by local fishermen and HM ships *Scourge* and *Heroic*. Although the largest vessel lost in the Great War – and a hospital ship – there was little media interest, being yet another casualty of the War.

WHITE
STAR
LINE

R.M.S. OLYMPIC 46,439 Tons
The largest British Steamer

Period postcard of *Olympic* acting as a troop transport. *Author's collection*

Olympic survived the conflict, having transported 201,000 troops and earning the nickname of 'Old Reliable'. In 1919 she was refitted; one of the first liners to be converted from coal to oil firing, during which a dent was found in her hull where a torpedo had failed to detonate. She returned to her Atlantic crossings, carrying numerous celebrities and royals along with her usual complement of hopeful emigrants. One such group moving to America was the Leach family. The young Archibald would become actor Cary Grant. She was involved in a couple more incidents; most serious being colliding with the Nantucket Lightship in fog in 1934, sinking the smaller wooden vessel with the loss of seven lives. More happily, in 1926 a passenger gave birth to a healthy boy, who was promptly given the name Olympic Valerie.

In 1934 White Star merged with Cunard. *Olympic* was now comparatively elderly, and in 1935 was withdrawn from service. Sold to Sir John Jarvis for £100,000, she last sailed under her own steam to Jarrow to be demolished, providing jobs for the area during the Depression. In 1937 the lower portion of her hull was towed to Inverkeithing for final scrapping. However, not everything was destroyed. All her interiors were stripped out and sold at auction, many remaining today – most notably at the White Swan Hotel in Alnwick.

WHITE STAR
LINE.

TRIPLE-SCREW R.M.S. "OLYMPIC."
46,359 TONS.
THE LARGEST BRITISH STEAMER.
PASSING AMBROSE CHANNEL LIGHTSHIP.

Period postcard of *Olympic* passing the Ambrose Lightship. *Author's collection*

Ismay resigned his post in 1913, becoming a director of the London Midland Scottish Railway Company upon its formation. Aiding many seafaring charities but keeping out of the public eye, he retired in the 1920s. Suffering from failing health, he died in 1937. Rostron would become Commodore of the Cunard line and later be knighted. He passed away in 1940. In 1947 Cunard bought out the remainder of White Star and, no longer using the name by 1960, the company ceased to exist.

Olympic off Southampton, dressed in flags. Author's collection

That *would* be the end of the story, were it not for *Titanic*. Interest has never waned, and many films have been made about her. Arguably the most significant is 'A Night to Remember'. This film remains the most historically accurate, not only through heavy research but because several survivors assisted with its production. The producer was none other than William MacQuitty, who had seen *Titanic* launched. With many of the films, however, the Inquiry's errors would perpetuate.

Ever since the sinking people had tried unsuccessfully to locate her wreck, from discussions by the Astors back in 1912 to oilman Jack Grimm's ill-fated expeditions of 1980-3. But in 1985 Doctor Robert Ballard of the Woods Hole Oceanographic Institute (and developer of the Remotely Operated Vehicle or ROV) was ordered by the American Navy to covertly record two Cold-War submarine wrecks. He was permitted as a cover story to use any spare time to search for *Titanic*. Working with a French team, who trawled the area with sonar (while Ballard investigated the submarines), on 1st September Ballard's ROV cameras sighted a boiler – *Titanic's* wreck was found.

Located at 41° 43' N, 49° 56' W, subsequent expeditions have recorded the condition of her wreck, identified historical and engineering aspects of the disaster and have recovered thousands of artefacts including her bell, personal items and even Major Peuchen's lost wallet.

Model of *Titanic's* bow section. David Lean

Much is still being learnt – for example biologists have discovered 27 new species of bacterial life on the wreck, one now named 'Halomonas Titanicae'. Many questions were answered by her discovery and many more raised, continually helping to fuel public interest.

Today the steward services on Cunard vessels are called the 'White Star Service', the last remnant of this once-proud company, and every 15th April the International Ice Patrol lay a wreath over the site in memory.

There is a Belfast saying: *Titanic* was not a disaster, what happened to her was. The fate that befell *Titanic* means that the Olympic Class will never be forgotten. But why all this fame? At no point was *Titanic* ever the worst maritime disaster in history. However, she was the first major disaster to be covered by international media. Her story has all the perfect ingredients: the rich and poor, famous and obscure, arrogance and horror. It was an extreme case of pride coming before a fall – mankind's greatest achievement falling victim to one of nature's simplest entities.

Conversely, some now wonder how other ships of her time may have coped in those conditions, suggesting that perhaps it is unfair to criticise so emphatically. Taking longer to sink than even her own designer expected, remaining stable and upright throughout, these factors gave precious time towards the evacuation. Therefore perhaps *Titanic* was indeed a safe ship, potentially saving lives even during her own demise. A highly contentious idea, this is just one of many aspects that will be debated long into the future.

Whatever the debates, one thing is certain. *Titanic* was a symbol of progress: social, technological but also quite literally a symbol of hope for those seeking a new life overseas. Faith, however, was shattered – not just faith in technology, but in a more general sense. *Titanic* heralded a change in era; the end of confidence and the start of more troubling times. To quote survivor Jack Thayer:

'There was peace and the world had an even tenor to its way. Nothing was revealed in the morning the trend of which was not known the night before. It seems to me that the disaster about to occur was the event that not only made the world rub its eyes and awake but woke it with a start keeping it moving at a rapidly accelerating pace ever since with less and less peace, satisfaction and happiness. To my mind the world of today awoke April 15th, 1912.'

Memorial to *Titanic's* Engineers, Southampton. *Author*

DEATH ON THE RAILS
The Quintinshill Fiasco

The period of World War One was full of tragedy, spawning events that remain in the collective imagination for their horror: Gallipoli, Flanders, the Somme. With troops marching across Europe, unprecedented zeppelin raids and the war at sea costing countless ships, civilians were increasingly in the crossfire. Of these, none would be more sadly infamous than those aboard RMS *Lusitania* when she was torpedoed and sunk in 1915. But scarcely three weeks after this act shocked the world, an incident occurred that was just as terrible – one that wiped out half a battalion in a matter of minutes. Astonishingly though, this major military loss had nothing to do with enemy action and, far from occurring in the heat of battle on foreign soil, it happened within earshot of the famed Scottish blacksmiths at romantic Gretna Green. A tragedy caused and worsened by forgetfulness, this was a disaster so startling that for the most part it was uncensored during the War. Still holding to this day the grim title of Britain's worst railway disaster, its name stands as a warning of the perils of distraction: Quintinshill.

Prior to the 1921 Grouping Act that formed the famous 'Big Four' railway

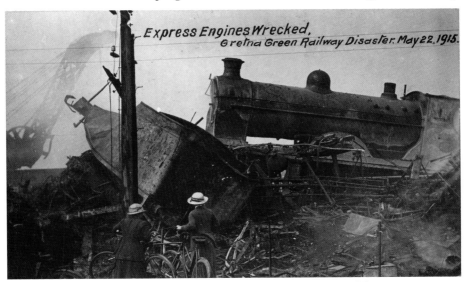

Period postcard showing the wrecked troop train tender and locomotive No. 140 of the Express.
Author's collection

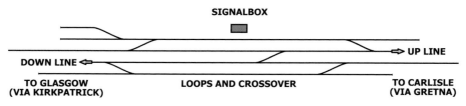

Track diagram for Quintinshill loops. *Author*

companies, Britain was criss-crossed with hundreds of small companies each owning varying amounts of track. For a long-distance non-stop journey a train would have to cross numerous companies' tracks, and with Expresses having priority over Goods trains, junctions where companies met frequently became massive bottlenecks. One such junction was the gateway to the north at Gretna; just south of Gretna Green, Scotland, shared by the Caledonian Railway Company and the Glasgow and South Western Railway. In order to alleviate difficulties, in the 1890s the Caledonian constructed a set of loops, siding and a signal box to the north, stretching between Blacksyke Bridge and the hamlet of Quintinshill.

Their operation was simple – Kirkpatrick signal box would contact the signalman at Quintinshill via telegraph to request permission (or 'offer') to send a train. The Quintinshill signalman would contact Gretna Junction signal box and see if the line ahead was clear. This is known as the 'Block System', allowing only one train on the stretch of track, or 'block' between signal boxes at a time. If clear, then the train could proceed uninterrupted. If not, or if there was a faster or higher priority train behind it, then the train could come to Quintinshill and wait in the loop until the line ahead was clear. With the main line itself free, Expresses could overtake if necessary, or another train could wait on the main line itself. Conversely, if no space was available then the train was refused. This process could happen for both lines – the 'up' line to Gretna and London and the 'down' line to Kirkpatrick and Glasgow each having a separate loop. The 'up' line is always the line to London, so in this case, heading south. There was also a private coal siding and a set of cross-over points enabling trains to change between the 'up' and 'down' lines if necessary.

With such a system there were various potential risks, so numerous safety features were incorporated. Firstly, regulations dictated that the signal box should only contain the signalman and that every action taken, or person bringing a message, should be written down in the Train Register Book – effectively a 'black box' record of movements. There were occasions when it was necessary, such as when the loops were occupied, to perform 'wrong line' shunting – transferring a train onto the opposite running line to permit another to pass. As this blocked the main line and was thus the most hazardous, this had a quadruple-layer safety system. Firstly there were the usual danger signals. Secondly, 'lever collars' were to be placed over the relevant signal levers, preventing them from accidentally being changed to green. Thirdly, the fireman of the train was to enter the signal box and remind the signalman of the train's presence – also checking the lever collars. Lastly, the signalman was to contact the preceding signalman and request him to set his block equipment to 'train on line'. A process called 'blocking back', this meant that the empty 'block' behind the stationary train was protected as well as the 'block' with the train itself.

On 22nd May 1915, the Caledonian Sleeper Express to Glasgow departed from Euston Station in, London. A joint train operated by the London and North Western Railway and the Caledonian, it paused at Carlisle to have the locomotives changed, gaining 'Dunalastair' class locomotives Nos. 48 and 140 (piloting) – the latter deemed necessary due to the weight of hauling 13 carriages over the gradient at Beattock. They were manned by Driver Johnstone, Fireman Graham, Driver Cowper and Fireman Todhunter respectively. In the process, however, it and its Edinburgh-bound counterpart were delayed by half an hour. Departing at 6:37am (instead of 6:05am as listed in the timetable), the so-named '6.5'

A lever collar in operation. *Author with permission from Didcot Railway Centre*

Express had been preceded by the 6:17am Caledonian Local to Beattock, known as the 'Parly' after the cheap Third Class trains brought about by the Parliamentary Railway Regulation Act of 1844. Although a minor train, it had to make the connection so departed at 6:10am (its official departure time), to be shunted at Quintinshill to allow the two Expresses to pass. Its locomotive was 'Cardean' class No. 907 – a surprisingly large engine for a train comprising only three carriages and a milk van. Its crew was Driver Wallace and Fireman Hutchinson.

Arriving at Gretna Junction, the engine gained a surreptitious passenger, strictly against regulations. James Tinsley aged thirty-two, was a signalman based at Quintinshill box. Officially he came on shift at 6:00am, however, he and his friend fellow Quintinshill signalman George Meakin aged thirty-one, had devised a system to gain half an hour in bed. Meakin and Tinsley's shifts crossed, so one would continue working after his shift officially ended until the other arrived. The isolated location of Quintinshill meant that no Station Master could check up on them. To complete the illusion of regular times, the Train Register Book would be left blank at 6:00am, with movements jotted down on the back of old forms, to be written up in the correct handwriting later. On the occasions when the Local was to be shunted it was even better, as Tinsley lived at Gretna so would have an easier journey. As on previous occasions, Tinsley crept along the far side of the engine and hid in the cab until they departed.

Arriving shortly before 6:30am, Tinsley immediately saw the situation at Quintinshill. Earlier, a 45 wagon Goods train had been shunted into the 'down' loop, preventing a simple shunt for the Local. Therefore, Meakin in the signal box

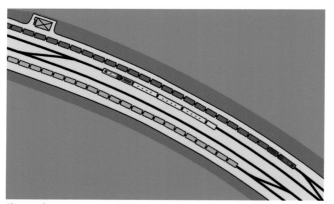

decided to 'wrong line' shunt the Local onto the 'up' line. Although with its risks, this had occurred four times in the last six months, so was a relatively familiar operation. As was common practice at Quintinshill – but against regulations – he did not use a lever collar. The Local came to a halt 63 yards from the

The Local train at Quintinshill stopped on the 'up' line; the Coal train in the upper loop and Goods train in the lower loop. *Author*

signal box. Furthermore, just before the local arrived an empty Naval Coal train pulled up on the 'up' line – stopped as Carlisle had no space for it. After dealing with the Local, Meakin put it in the 'up' loop, before accepting the Edinburgh Express via the telegraph. Tinsley came up to the signal box and at 6:32am came on duty.

Around this time Brakeman Ingram of the Goods train came up for a chat, failing to either sign the Register – the official purpose for visiting the box – or promptly leave. Tinsley discussed train movements with Meakin before reading through the scraps to be written up into the Register. At 6:34am a message came through that a special Troop train passed Lockerbie two minutes earlier. Meakin replaced the points and signals behind the Coal train. Kirkpatrick box received the message 'train out of section' for the Coal train. However, it is unknown which signalman sent it – Meakin being the more likely. He did not 'block back' the Local, later claiming this was because the Coal train was still on the main line and that afterwards he was off duty. Nonetheless it was his duty to complete the movements for the train he shunted. He did not remind Tinsley. He properly handed over operations, before taking Tinsley's newspaper and thumbing through the War news.

As this took place, another train was heading south towards Quintinshill. Called to join the 52nd Lowland Division as reinforcements for the Gallipoli campaign, the 1/7th Royal Scots battalion from Leith was to move on 19th May. However, their transport

A coach similar to those in the Troop train.
Author with permission from the Buckinghamshire Railway Centre

– HMT *Aquitania* – had struck a sandbank off Liverpool, delaying plans. At 3:30am on the 22nd, three trains departed from Larbert Station bound for Liverpool. The first contained the Commanding Officers and HQ plus the main body of soldiers – eight to a compartment. The second carried the other half of the battalion, and the last carried horses and their equipment. With the railways hard-pressed for rolling stock owing to the increasing number of war-time trains, this first train comprised 15 old wooden-bodied carriages and vans borrowed from the Great Central Railway. They would have been scrapped had the War not started. 12 were gas-lit, ironically using a German system. The locomotive was 'Dunalastair' class No. 121, crewed by Driver Scott and Fireman Hannah. They had some difficulties keeping to time, taking sixty-five minutes to pass Lockerbie, and were some minutes late. However, such 'Specials' were ordered to take priority over any other train. As they neared Quintinshill Scott picked up speed down the gradient, averaging roughly 70mph.

Back at the signal box Meakin and Brakeman Ingram were discussing the paper while Tinsley started to write up his books. At 6:35am Fireman Hutchinson of the Local came up to remind Tinsley about his train (as regulations dictated). He signed the book in a blank section to be filled out later, but did not query his train's position, as Tinsley had travelled with him and assured him that he knew where the Local was. He did not ask for a lever collar. Then instead of leaving, Hutchinson joined Meakin and Ingram with the newspaper. Shortly afterwards they were joined by Brakeman Young of the Coal train, who came to query his relief but never actually got around to mentioning it – instead joining the others. As is apparent, the rule of the signalman having to remain alone was overlooked – Quintinshill box even having a reputation as a social gathering place. After a minute or two, Hutchinson returned to the Local, Ingram to the Goods train, and at 6:38am the Edinburgh Express passed through on the 'down' line. Unusually, Caledonian signal boxes were so arranged that to operate the levers and 'block' instruments, the signalman had to have his back to the windows and trains.

The footplate of 1917-built No. 5322, showing limited visibility on curved track akin to Quintinshill. *Author with permission from Didcot Railway Centre*

To recap: the signal box which should have contained just Tinsley held three people. Tinsley was concentrating on writing up the Train Register. The Local train was standing on the wrong 'up' line with signals set to danger to protect it. There were no lever collars locking the signals and the train had not been 'blocked back'. At 6:42am, Kirkpatrick telegraphed offering the Troop train on the 'up' line. Tinsley accepted. He offered it to Gretna, who accepted. Tinsley heard the block bell ring to say 'train entering section'. Gretna offered him the '6.5' Express (travelling on the 'down' line). He accepted. He never looked out of the window at the large blue locomotive outside. He cleared all the 'up' signals to green.

As Meakin walked out onto the signal box steps at 6:50am to start his way home, he saw the Troop train tearing down the line. He shouted to Tinsley:

'Whatever have you done, Jimmy?'

'Good heavens! What can be wrong? The frame's all right and the signals are all right.'

'You have got the 'Parly' standing there!'

Fireman Hutchinson, having previously returned to his engine, was just opening his sandwich tin when he saw the signals were cleared. He noted it to

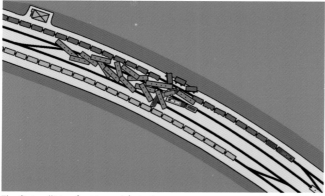

The first collision (not to scale). *Author*

Driver Wallace, who suddenly saw the Troop train coming round the curve towards them. Each man dove off the footplate and rolled under the nearest truck of the two freight trains. The northern end of the loops is by an over-bridge, Blacksyke Bridge, and the line curves to the right. Lined either side by the freight trains, forward visibility from the Troop train engine would have been near zero. Scott and Hannah would only have seen the local at a distance of 285 yards. Adding the necessity to perform duties other than just watching, they had no chance of avoiding calamity. Travelling at 70mph, it is believed they managed to slow down to about 40mph. However, even at this reduced speed a 500-ton train encountering a 200-ton obstacle could only have one result.

Mechanically speaking, the collision was massive. No. 907 on the Local suffered severe front end damage and was forced back 42 yards, derailing. The carriages partially telescoped, crumpling into each other, propelling them and the van 100 yards along the track where they were brought to a halt. Both freight trains received damage as wreckage struck them. The Troop train, however bore the brunt of the collision. No. 121 was thrown across the 'up' line on its side, its tender landing across the 'down' line. The investigation's damage summary demonstrates how powerful the forces involved were:

> *'Engine No. 121 (of Troop Train) – Engine framing broken and bent; buffer-beam knocked off; bogie displaced and destroyed; driving wheels bent; engine cylinders broken; engine motion-plate bent; connecting rods bent; eccentric rods bent; engine coupling-rods bent; smoke-box knocked inwards and wrecked; brake gearing broken off; cab framing wrecked; ashpan-casting broken off; firebars displaced. Tender wrecked.'*

The forward carriages crumpled, mounted the engine and catapulted over it, some landing level with the Local's tender. A few vans at the rear broke free and recoiled up the gradient, being stopped by Brakeman Young of the Goods train. The rest of the train was scattered across both running lines; carriages breaking apart, scattering debris. Originally a length of 215 yards, the wrecked Troop train was only 67 yards long.

But survivor accounts suggest that this collision was by no means as fatal as the damage would indicate. In the Local, two passengers were killed when the first carriage telescoped. Scott and Hannah of the Troop train locomotive would have been killed instantly. Many soldiers undoubtedly perished, but accounts show that within seconds of impact soldiers were clambering out of the wreckage. Many even survived from the forward carriages – soaked with water from the tender and thrown through the air having taking the brunt of the collision. Most only had slight

Period postcard of the crushed Local train coaches. *Author's collection*

injuries – primarily caused by their rifles falling from the luggage racks – but some were trapped in the shattered carriages, or were slow in extricating themselves from the wreckage due to injuries. Their comrades ran back across the tracks to assist. Others went to help the Local's passengers. It was a most serious accident, but it was far from over. In the few seconds after the collision, Meakin and Tinsley stood at the signal box steps and watched the two trains pile up before them. Before running down the steps to help, Meakin shouted to Tinsley again:

'Where is the 6.5?'

Seeing that nothing in his power could be done, Meakin quickly returned to the box. Tinsley stood by the lever frame, but had not set the signals to danger. Meakin had to do it. Driver Wallace of the Local crawled out from under a truck and saw the 'down' signals still set to clear. He called to soldiers to clear the tracks, but was not heard. Guard Graham of the Local and Driver Benson and Fireman Grierson of the Coal train ran down the line as fast as they could – 167 yards in 40 seconds it was calculated – waving their arms violently. All saw the same thing: the '6.5' Express thundering towards the wreckage. It had passed the signals *before* they were set to danger.

Fireman Todhunter of the Express's pilot engine late recounted:

'…on approaching Quintinshill the signals were all clear for us. The first notice of anything being wrong was when approaching the home signal, when I observed a guard waving his arms as if something was the matter. I shouted to my driver to stop, as I saw there was something in front. He came from his side of the engine to my side and immediately applied the brakes, shut off steam, and endeavoured to stop as hard as he could.'

Driver Cowper continued:

'On looking up I saw the wreckage in front of me, and in a few seconds we struck it. The first collision was not very hard, and there was a great sound of splintering wood and breaking glass followed by a very hard blow which almost brought us to a stand. I was buried up to the neck in the left-hand corner of my engine cab by the coals from the tender, with my back to the fire-box. I was assisted out by driver Johnston and my own fireman, and was considerably bruised and somewhat burned about the neck. I was also somewhat stunned, but had my wounds dressed on the field, and was able to assist some of the wounded.'

The Express barely had time to slow down; the curve of the line again hindering forward visibility till too late. Travelling at 50mph, the drivers were able to reduce speed to 40mph when the train struck the forward Troop train carriages – the 'splintered wood' described by Cowper. Although acting as a cushion, the Express tore through it and unfortunate soldiers before striking the tender of No. 121, ploughing it through the wreckage into the Goods train. No. 140 was de-railed and also forced into the Goods train, while its tender mounted No. 48's buffer beam – the latter's tender resting against No. 907 of the Local. The first four carriages of the Express partly

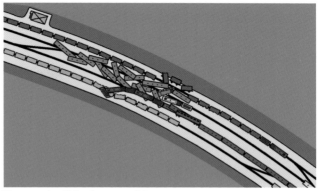

The second collision (not to scale). *Author*

telescoped; the second falling on its side, and only the fourth remaining on the rails. The duration between the two collisions was 53 seconds.

Six were killed on the Express; two further mortally injured. It is unknown how many from the Troop train were killed in this second collision, as the disaster was still unfurling.

The two collisions had decimated the old carriages of the Troop train, but had also ruptured their lighting reservoirs which had been fully charged – gas

TERRIBLE TROOP TRAIN DISASTER.
One of the express engines telescoped on top of the wreckage of the troop train. The tender (on the left) has been thrown right over the side of the track.

Period postcard depicting No. 140 of the Express and the mangled Troop train's tender. *Author's collection*

escaping rapidly. Almost instantly the wreckage burst into flames. Driver Moss of the Goods train uncoupled the first 33 trucks and pulled them clear of the fire. Returning, the Express and Coal train crews desperately tried to douse the conflagration with water from their tenders, but there was little left and no way to fight it effectively, particularly as undamaged gas cylinders started to explode.

At this point, the telephone rang in the signal box – it was Gretna signal box, enquiring where the Troop train was. Tinsley calmly replied *'We have had a smash up here'* and put the phone down. Gretna phoned again, Tinsley – now frantically shouting – replied:

> *'Send for the platelayers, send for the stationmaster, send for **everybody**!'*

Period postcard depicting the burning Express.
Author's collection

Tinsley sent the 'obstruction danger' signal both ways, then extraordinarily completed regular operational procedure by signalling 'train entering section' for the Express burning furiously outside. The time was 6:53am. Three minutes had elapsed. Describing the scene, a reporter said:

'In a moment all was terrible confusion. Engines were heaped upon one another, carriages telescoped and overturned, and others mounted one upon the other. Men were hurled from the train – a fortunate few well clear – others clambered out from the wreckage as best they could. Many were pinned below the overturned carriages. Already the troop train and the leading carriages of the London train were ablaze. The men still on board were in a terrible plight. The successive collisions had effectively jammed the carriage doors. Exit that way was impossible. Windows refused to come down, and the glass had to be smashed before the men could get clear. Many men confessed that they did not know by what means or in what manner they got out. "The great this is, we got out" said one man, "and we thank God we got clear of yon hell".'

Many were less fortunate. The flames were so hot that the steel of the Express carriages buckled and twisted 'like drying leaves', and few attempted to fight the fire – recognising it as uncontrollable. For those still trapped there were few options. Later interviews recorded some using their bayonets to perform self-amputations, others cutting their own throats with jack-knives, while a group of comrades begged an Officer to shoot them. The Officer complied. Despite some Press reports to the contrary, most accounts suggest that many were still alive and conscious when the flames enveloped them – *'insistent and heart-rending cries for help had in many cases to go unheeded, so terrible was the fire'*. Small

The burned-out Express sleeper car. © *The British Library*, The Daily Sketch, *24 May 1915, p.1*

surprise that *The Times* referred to the disaster as 'worse than in the trenches'. As a surviving soldier put it:

> *'I would far rather be out in Flanders – you do get a run for your money there.'*

The Gretna signalman informed Stationmaster Thorburn, who ran up the line, joining two other railwaymen and various locals who all heard the crashes and saw the smoke. Thorburn immediately began to coordinate the rescue. The undamaged portions of the Express were drawn clear and the Goods train's engine sent to get carriages to take away the uninjured. Word got to Gretna Green via the caretaker of the famous blacksmiths, who heard the crash and thought it was the Germans. Local medical personnel quickly arrived and assisted the injured – performing rudimentary amputations with carpentry saws on some to release them, all being placed in the adjoining field where many died from shock. At 7:14am Carlisle Station was informed, assembling a special Ambulance train which arrived at the scene by 8:10am. Amazingly, no-one thought about informing Carlisle Fire Brigade, who initially heard that the fire was extinguished. Later they were told otherwise and arrived at 8:55am – far too late to control the flames. When the Caledonian Railway Headquarters at Glasgow were informed they made up a Special train of doctors and railway officials. When they arrived they found Tinsley and Meakin still in their box. Assistant Superintendent Killin asked Tinsley *'How on earth did it happen?'* Tinsley just replied:

> *'I forgot about the Local being on the up line and brought on the Troop train.'*

More doctors drove from Glasgow and Edinburgh, and Red Cross personnel informed by the Fire Brigade also arrived, as did many locals. Soldiers ran to get tools from the detached rear vans, while a group of sailors from the Express assisted fellow passengers. The first 52 injured were put aboard the intact portion of the Express and taken to Carlisle's Cumberland Infirmary, arriving at 10:42am. Two more trains followed, with most of the injured cleared by mid-day. Having just received a batch of wounded from France, Carlisle was over-

Assisting wounded in the fields. © *The British Library,*
The Daily Sketch, *24 May 1915, p.8*

Doctors arriving on-scene by car. © *The British Library,*
The Daily Sketch, *24 May 1915, p.9*

whelmed – some being treated in the street – so the less serious were moved on to Preston and Penrith Hospitals. The Red Cross commandeered several hotels and schools to deal with the injured, along with volunteers from the increasing number of onlookers. At 4:00pm, Colonel Peebles had a roll call of Royal Scots. The Battalion rolls were destroyed in the fire, so he took down names. Having left Larbert with 470 men and 15 officers, he counted 67 uninjured men – only five from 'A' Company. At 4:30pm they marched into Carlisle.

Having been relieved of duties, Meakin went to the local pub (owned by his

THE RAILWAY DISASTER NEAR CARLISLE.
A roll of the troops was called at 11.30. Fifty-two men of the Royal Scots answered the roll
call out of about 500. A large number of the survivors accompanied their wounded comrades to
the hospital, and the roll call was in consequence incomplete. The photo shows the calling
of the roll.

Period postcard showing the roll call of surviving Royal Scots soldiers. *Author's collection*

Clearing the wreckage. © *The British Library*, The Daily Sketch, *24 May 1915, pp.8-9*

wife), finding that owing to so many coming to see the disaster it was virtually out of beer. He and a friend drove to the village to order some more, running down a young boy on their return. Expecting to go on duty the next day (Sunday), he was surprised to hear he had been suspended – he considered Tinsley to be solely at fault.

On the Sunday, back at the scene, the Fire Brigade left – the fire had burnt for twenty-three hours. Bodies were recovered from the ashes; virtually all unidentifiable. The last was recovered at mid-day, but as the breakdown gangs cleared the line they found a single foot, which they buried by the lineside. At 8:14pm the line reopened. Engines No. 907 and 121 were irreparable, and most of the carriages were totally destroyed.

Period postcard showing the result of the fire. *Author's collection*

It was calculated that from the 1/7th Royal Scots, 83 were killed and identified, and 50 posted as 'missing' (one later found as having been sent on leave from hospital). There were 82 unidentified victims; the majority probably soldiers. Of the survivors, only Colonel Peebles and six officers were declared fit for active service. In the course of three minutes, half a battalion had been wiped out.

In total from the three trains, the disaster injured 246 and killed 226 – a grim record.

In the aftermath the Press initially wrote little, however, as the magnitude came to be known it became front-page news with surprisingly little censorship. There was also indignation that nothing had been learnt from previous fire-based accidents such as at Hawes Junction (1910) and Ais Gill (1913). In Leith and Carlisle the lists of casualties were read out (a train being provided to take relatives to the hospitals – 20 or so travelling in vain), and the recovered bodies were taken to Leith by train. The surviving soldiers were sent to Liverpool before their superiors realised they were not fit to fight. Unsurprisingly they were reticent about travelling by train. When met at Liverpool by the Sergeant-Major from the other half of the Battalion, on the un-involved second Troop train, the sight made him break down. One can only imagine their appearance – local children threw stones, thinking them to be POWs. They returned to Edinburgh, and were present when their fallen comrades were buried in Rosebank Cemetery near Leith after a three-hour funeral procession lined with crowds. The 'fit' officers and remaining half of the Battalion not involved in the disaster were shipped out to Gallipoli, where by mid-July only 174 were left out of the 1,028 that had originally departed from Larbert.

FUNERAL OF 100 VICTIMS OF THE GRETNA GREEN RAILWAY DISASTER AT LEITH WITH MILITARY HONOURS.
The long line of transport waggons containing the coffins passing through the town to the cemetery.

Period postcard of the Royal Scots' funeral procession. *Author's collection*

From the moment the railway officials arrived and spoke to Tinsley and Meakin, a full Caledonian Railway investigation started, followed by a Board of Trade Inquiry led by Colonel Druitt. But unlike most accidents, Druitt saw no fault with railway equipment other than noting the risk of fire from gas-lighting; referring back to previous accidents involving the system. The cause was clear from the start. The only potential factor was the lack of new 'track circuit' technology to electrically locate a train's position. But as such a minor location with a near prefect view of the line, Quintinshill box would have been one of the last to receive it. As it was apparent that a trial was likely, publication of the report (and final death count) was withheld. Compensation was paid by the Caledonian to Scott and Hannah's widows, and to the Great Central Railway who owned the carriages. Some passengers threatened to sue, receiving small sums.

On 29th May, Tinsley was arrested for culpable homicide and taken to Dumfries Prison, but later released on bail. He was the only one indicted when the Coroners' Inquiry was held. Scottish law does not have these Inquiries; however, as 26 victims died in Carlisle the disaster was unusual in coming under both Scottish and English jurisdiction.

The wounded being tended to. © *The British Library*, The Daily Sketch, *24 May 1915, p.9*

Cross-examined on all aspects of the disaster, from the shift changes to each person's actions, Coroner Strong made it clear that he considered Hutchinson partly responsible. The Jury gave a verdict of 'Gross Negligence' – taken by Strong as manslaughter. The verdict was unanimous for Meakin and Tinsley, but 12 to seven for Hutchinson; Strong considered this sufficient. Their solicitor queried the legitimacy of his power as the accident was Scottish. Strong replied that the Home Office supported it under the Coroner's Act of 1887 – permitting investigation even if the act occurred outside England. Tinsley thus became one of few, if not the only person to be charged twice for the same crime – culpable homicide in Scotland and manslaughter in England. Committed to the Cumberland Assizes, all three men were arrested and bailed. It was later decided that the case would be heard at the next Assizes, so the case returned to the Scottish High Court in Edinburgh.

On 24th September the trial commenced, with Tinsley, Meakin and Hutchinson all in the dock. Each charge was read out: Meakin primarily responsible for failing to 'block back' or use lever collars, Hutchinson failing to ensure the above and Tinsley for accepting the Troop train. They were also charged with the fact that these failures of duty led to the deaths of many. They pleaded 'Not Guilty'. Following the outline of the Coroner's Inquest, experts were called and those involved examined. No defence witnesses were called. It was recognised that Hutchinson was not culpable, but under Scottish procedure he had to remain in the dock. The Lord Advocate's case summarised by stating:

'I think you would agree that it would be quite intolerable if these valuable human lives, dear to their friends and invaluable to their country at the moment when it happened, should be imperilled and sacrificed.

Why?

In order that a signalman may spend half an hour more between the sheets on a particular morning.

My suggestion is that if that arrangement had not existed none of us would be here today and much valuable life would have been preserved. A verdict in favour of the accused would be rightly interpreted as a character of indemnity to

railway officials to disregard the rules provided by the company if they so please.
My painful but clear duty is to ask you to return a verdict of guilty as
libelled.'

While the Defence inferred that this speech was prejudiced against the men,
it failed to stand up – especially as the Defending Counsel had a poor grasp of
railway procedure and, however innocent the motives, it was a clear case of
neglect. The trial lasted one and a half days, culminating in a damning summary
by Lord Strathclyde. The Jury retired for eight minutes and unanimously found
Meakin and Tinsley guilty, but asked for leniency as both men's health had
deteriorated near to mental breakdown. Meakin was sentenced to eighteen
months; Tinsley to three years. Some railwaymen petitioned to have these
reduced, but their argument of 'wartime conditions' fell flat. There was a final
inquiry for Scott, Hannah and Samuel Dyer (a sleeping car attendant representing all the victims), which concluded that:

'If the regulations of the railway company had been followed the accident
would not have happened.'

Meakin and Tinsley were released after twelve months, partly on medical
grounds and partly through involvement on their behalf by the National Union

of Railwaymen. Re-joining the
Caledonian Railway, Tinsley became a
lampman at Carlisle. He died in 1967.
Meakin became a coal merchant – out
of Quintinshill siding – and later
worked in Gretna Munitions Factory.
He died in 1950. Today the signal box
is long gone but, although infre-
quently used, the loops are still
present. At Larbert Station is a
memorial to the 1/7th Royal Scots,
while opposite Gretna's famous blacksmiths stands a memorial to all those
lost. In 2010 a plaque was unveiled on
Blacksyke Bridge overlooking the site.
Additional memorials were also
created for the centenary and the
tragedy finally received some of the
national recognition it had grimly
earned.

Quintinshill today, viewed from Blacksyke Bridge
looking south. *James T M Towill, Creative Commons*
Attribution-Share Alike 2.0 license

Why did it happen? Tinsley and
Meakin's shift-rigging was seen by

many as the central cause, as even allowing for smaller regulations being ignored, Tinsley's attention was fully taken by writing up the Register to hide their scheme, instead of on his work. Furthermore, *had* the book been complete, Hutchinson's signature would have acted as yet another reminder. But this is by no means the sole reason.

Meakin performed a risky shunting operation with the Local and failed to 'block back' or use a lever collar. The former was apparently due to him changing over with Tinsley in the middle of the Coal train movements and was an uncommon omission. The lack of lever collars, however, was a *daily* failure – another case of slackness with regulations. In any event, it was Meakin's fault these were not done, not Tinsley's:

THE RAILWAY DISASTER NEAR CARLISLE.
ALL THAT REMAINED OF THE SLEEPING CAR.

Period postcard depicting the burned-out Express.
Author's collection

> '*Was it your* [Meakin's] *duty or was it not, to put the lever collar on the home signal when you put the obstruction on the line?'*
> '*Yes.'*

These two safety devices cannot be under-played in significance; to quote Tinsley's examination:

> '*If the lever collar had been on the lever of the home signal there would have been no accident?'*
> '*It could not have happened.'*

> '*If the blocking back signal had been given there would have been no accident?'*
> '*No.'*

But why did he stop mid-way through manoeuvres? He wanted to read the newspaper. When others came to the box, it was a good chance for a chat. To quote Meakin at the inquiry, '*we were all talking together*'. While the lone Tinsley should have awaited notifications of train movements, in reality he was absorbed in copying up the Train Register Book while his friends chatted about the news. This was hardly conducive to concentration – demonstrated by the fact that no-one could remember who exactly did what.

Hutchinson failed to expressly remind Tinsley about his train, but as Tinsley had left his engine barely minutes beforehand, this failure is understandable. Not querying the lack of lever collars was more serious, but again a result of the infrequency with which they were used in spite of regulations to the contrary.

Remains of the Goods train. © *The British Library*, The Daily Sketch, *24 May 1915, p.8*

Particularly as Meakin had (theoretically) dealt with the Local, Tinsley simply forgot about it. Never looking out of the window, he never questioned what his instruments told him and set the signals to green.

There have been recent claims that Tinsley suffered from epilepsy and the Caledonian subsequently effected a 'conspiracy' to hide this medical condition during the Inquiry, as it would have placed blame with the Caledonian for employing him as a signalman. Potentially explaining the final error and his actions in the aftermath, the epilepsy claim is only circumstantial and effectively unprovable, while the latter 'conspiracy' is improbable. Even if there was 'damage limitation' by the Caledonian, this was commonplace for the time – as

FUNERAL OF 100 VICTIMS OF THE GRETNA GREEN RAILWAY DISASTER AT LEITH WITH MILITARY HONOURS.
The procession on the way to the cemetery headed by bagpipes and muffled drums.

Period postcard of pipers in the Royal Scots funeral procession. *Author's collection* examples, both *Titanic* and *Lusitania* were subject to this in their aftermaths – and cannot be used as any real evidence of a cover-up. In any event, the 'conspiracy' still fails to excuse ignoring regulations and multiple failings that would have protected the train even if Tinsley *had* suffered an epileptic fit, much less the equally-faulty actions of Meakin. Ultimately, how Tinsley could forget a train he just got off will never be known or understood.

Lost in friendly fields... © *The British Library*, The Daily Sketch, *24 May 1915, p.16*

After the first collision, Meakin immediately remembered the '6.5' Express and shouted to Tinsley. Running to help but swiftly returning, he found Tinsley still standing there, likely suffering from shock (if not also the residual effects of epilepsy). Those few seconds delay possibly caused the second collision; there may well have been time to brake otherwise. As for the fire, that was unavoidable even after just the first collision, and the age and construction of the carriages only worsened the situation.

So what was the ultimate cause of the Quintinshill tragedy? The simple answer is laxity. Had regulations been obeyed then it was avoidable. Had lever collars been used it would not have happened. Had the change-over occurred at the correct time, without a desire for additional sleep, then the Register would not have distracted them, and the 'blocking back' in all probability would have been remembered. Had the brakemen not visited to read the paper, coupled with the other distractions mentioned, then the Local may not have been forgotten. To err is human, and it would have been unfortunate timing if Tinsley had been afflicted with an epileptic attack at that crucial moment, but had regulations been obeyed by any of those involved then it would not have mattered and the Troop train would have come to a safe halt.

Three men were lax and 226 died.

But Meakin and Tinsley paid heavily for their actions. To quote historian Tom Rolt: '*Surely they are to be pitied rather than blamed, for have we not all been equally careless and forgetful on occasion but with no such fearful result?*'

Therein lies the tragedy of Quintinshill.

The Rosebank Cemetery memorial to the Quintinshill Royal Scot victims, Edinburgh. *Kim Traynor, Creative Commons Attribution-Share Alike 3.0 license*

'ALMOST INCONCEIVABLE NEGLIGENCE'
The *Lusitania* Debacle

Throughout history mankind has been plagued by disaster – often of his own making. When occuring because of war it is mostly ignored or written off as 'collateral damage', either as there is more 'important' news or it is feared the event may damage morale. So for a wartime event to be publicly considered 'disastrous' it must have significant importance, such as severity or propaganda value. But while news of such events is frequently simplified in their causes, invariably placing sole blame on the enemy 'perpetrator', this is seldom the full picture, and on occasion even the aggrieved nation must take some of the blame.

During World War One the 'rules of war' changed and non-combatant civilians began to find themselves directly in the line of fire, be it from airship attack, naval bombardment, or as passengers on the high seas. Easily the best remembered ship attack during the 'Great War', the torpedoing of the Cunard flagship RMS *Lusitania* remains a highly sensitive event – a propaganda boon for Britain and America that has since been over-credited with importance and subject to myth and intrigue. From the moment news broke of the huge loss of life, the submarine commander and Germany as a whole would be entirely

Period postcard of the newly-completed *Lusitania*. *David Lean collection*

blamed for the disaster, and pilloried for this 'barbaric' act. As Admiralty Wreck Commissioner Lord Mersey concluded at the *Lusitania* Inquiry:

'The whole blame for the cruel destruction of life in this catastrophe must rest solely with those who plotted and with those who committed the crime.'

However, this simple statement is far from the case. Many questions have been raised about her crew, cargo and the circumstances of her voyage, while her commander was initially accused of 'almost inconceivable negligence' by Captain Webb of the British Admiralty Trade Division. Some have even argued that these accusations attempted to draw blame away from the Admiralty, the central players in a purported international conspiracy. As an act described as 'wilful murder', who *really* should be blamed for the sinking of *Lusitania*?

Lusitania's origins lie well before her construction. German unification in 1871 and the coronation of Kaiser Wilhelm II created a great sense of national pride, and as a new nation state they wished to put their mark on everything – including at sea. Their new liner *Kaiser Wilhelm der Grosse*, the largest and fastest vessel in the world, took the 'Blue Riband' speed record from the Cunard liner *Lucania* in 1897, and was considered superior to any British liner in both speed and luxury, creating increasingly-fierce rivalry between shipping companies. Then in 1902 the White Star Line was amalgamated into the International Mercantile Marine Company. With this major British company now essentially American-owned, the British Admiralty feared that should war be declared they would not be able to requisition enough British-owned merchantmen for naval duty. As a direct result, Cunard and the British Government discussed building two new liners: to be the largest, fastest and most luxurious, but also capable of carrying substantial weaponry. The Government loaned Cunard £2,600,000 to construct them on the condition that in wartime they would be immediately converted to 'Armed Merchant Cruisers'.

Named *Lusitania* and *Mauretania* after Roman provinces, they were designed to be revolutionary and include distinctly naval features. Constructed at the John Brown shipyard at Clydebank, *Lusitania* was launched on 6th June 1906 amid great publicity. Compared to other ships of the period she had a near-completely original design – *The New York Times* calling her 'the greatest steamship ever built', and 'as unsink-able as a ship can be'. At 787 feet long, she was propelled by four high-pressure steam turbines – their first large-scale use – giving a top speed of 26 knots. Built primarily for the

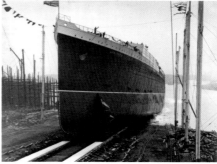

Lusitania's launch. *Eric Sauder Collection*

emigrant trade, many passengers from the three classes on board commented on her luxurious interiors and services available. Some aspects, however, such as her bulkheads and narrow width owed more to warship development. Indeed, internationally available lists of naval vessels listed *Lusitania* as an 'Armed Auxiliary Cruiser', and her plans indicated potential positions for six-inch guns.

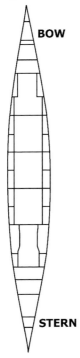

BOW

STERN

Diagram of *Lusitania's* watertight compartments (note the longitudinal divisions lining the central boiler and engine rooms).
Author

However, design issues arose from the Admiralty's interference. Originally to have been built with a beam (width) of 78 feet, model tests by chief designer Leonard Peskett indicated tremendous instability. The Admiralty subsequently permitted a maximum width of 87 feet six inches, forcing her to be taller in order to fit all the requirements made by both them and Cunard. As a result, she became one of the tallest ships yet constructed at that point, but this raised her centre of gravity.

Related to this issue, her bulkheads were increasingly found to be problematic. *Lusitania* was divided internally into 14 principal compartments using transverse bulkheads running from one side of the ship to the other and, using a basic naval defensive design, had additional bulkheads running longitudinally from bow to stern either side of her boiler and engine rooms. This subdividing resulted in a total of 34 sub-compartments, with 20 (ten either side) shielding her machinery areas. These compartments were to be used as coal bunkers with water-tight doors. Theoretically this meant in the event of a collision, mine or torpedo rupturing the hull, her boilers would be protected by effectively a second skin, coal also being perceived as a shock absorber, and she could thus survive.

But using longitudinal compartments as coal bunkers had already begun to be questioned, as the bunker openings in them made them no longer watertight. It was well known that coal often blocked the doors, jamming them open so rendering them useless – in 1886 the Cunard liner *Oregon* had sunk as a direct result of this after a collision. Various special Board of Trade Committees were held over the following decades, ultimately being reticent of this system as they also feared that any flooding would massively compromise stability, forcing any vessel to list. Before construction Peskett had already worryingly calculated (also considering the effect on general stability of her raised centre of gravity) that should one bunker flood *Lusitania* would list seven degrees; water in two bunkers 15 degrees, and three bunkers flooded would probably sink her. The captain's manual even stated that should she list over 22 degrees and not recover then she was to be immediately abandoned.

After the loss of *Titanic*, further discussions aired active criticism – naval architect Edward Wilding openly objecting to such longitudinal partitions, also noting that the resultant list would hinder lowering lifeboats. Indeed, he specifically called such a design 'dangerous'. Direct comparisons were made with *Lusitania* throughout the Inquiries and Peskett patently knew of these issues; to quote him at the British *Titanic* Inquiry:

> 21202. *Now with regard to counteracting the list which might arise from the longitudinal watertight compartments; you propose to do that by a system of counteracting flooding on the other side?*
> - *That is so, yes.*
> 21203. *That is a rather ticklish operation, is it not?*
> - *No.*
> *Well, you say no in a doubtful sort of way.*
> 21204. *(The Commissioner.) You do; you say it in what I call a speculative tone of voice. Have you ever known it put in practice?*
> - *I have never known it, no. I hope not.*

Worse still, at the start of the conflict an event occurred that conclusively proved that longitudinal bulkheads were not only no defence but a major liability. On 22nd September 1914, HM Ships *Aboukir*, *Cressy* and *Hogue* were sailing off the Dutch coast. Old outmoded cruisers with inexperienced crews, they had been nicknamed the 'Livebait Squadron'. At 6:20am *Aboukir* suffered an explosion and stopped dead. Assuming a mine, Captain Drummond ordered the other vessels to assist. Losing power, flooding in her starboard longitudinal compartments made her list violently, *Aboukir* capsizing and sinking in 25 minutes with only one lifeboat launched. As *Hogue* and *Cressy* slowed to assist, a submarine was spotted surfacing: the *U-9* under the command of Kapitänleutnant Otto Weddigen. *Hogue* opened fire but it dived, having fired two further torpedoes. *Hogue* was struck and sank in fifteen minutes – again capsizing. *Cressy* attempted to ram the *U-9*, but was itself struck by yet a further two torpedoes. Capsizing rapidly, she sank in twenty-five minutes. Three vessels and around 1450 sailors – more than at the Battle of Trafalgar – were lost in only one hour, thirty-five minutes.

A massive embarrassment for the Royal Navy, Otto Weddigen became a German hero and a source of much propaganda and publicity. More widely, he singlehandedly proved that the U-boat was not only useful as a reconnaissance tool, but that these mere 'toys' had a very real and powerful capacity for aggressive use – something that would transform war at sea forever. As is plain, the loss of stability in each of these vessels through unbalanced flooding resulted

Lusitania on her sea trials. *Eric Sauder Collection*

in rapid capsizing and sinking, and as such longitudinal bulkheads were actually extremely vulnerable to torpedo attack.

As far as *Lusitania* was concerned, partly with hindsight but nonetheless with aspects known beforehand, these interconnected stability and bulkhead issues were fundamental dangers before she had even been built. The public, though, had no knowledge of any flaws. In peacetime, accidents notwithstanding, these should not have been anything more than theoretical issues and no real significance was apparently put on these faults – attention concentrating on her revolutionary nature.

In July 1907 *Lusitania* underwent her sea trials, and was passed as seaworthy with no hesitation. Then came her acceptance trials before officially becoming part of the Cunard fleet – a mere formality. Shockingly, she failed. Her revolutionary engines, emphasised by four closely-set propellers, caused such powerful vibrations that most stern Second Class cabins were essentially uninhabitable. As a result her stern was gutted and her structure braced and stiffened before the cabins were refitted. Only by late August was she finally accepted by Cunard, although the vibration issue was never fully resolved.

Lusitania sailed on her maiden voyage on 7th September 1907, arriving triumphant in New York in five days fifty-four minutes, while on her second

Maiden voyage arrival in New York.
Eric Sauder Collection

voyage she regained the 'Blue Riband' trophy with a speed of 24 knots – her voyage lasting four days, nineteen hours and fifty-three minutes. Later in her career she would beat her own record three times. After entering service in November 1907 her sister *Mauretania* made another new record, and with some modifications increasing her tonnage became the largest vessel afloat. White Star quickly realised they were losing clientele to Cunard, so as a consequence constructed two 'Olympic' Class liners. While *Olympic* was to be highly successful, *Titanic* sent shockwaves through the industry and influenced international legislation. Cunard recalled *Lusitania* mid-1912 to fit additional lifeboats to meet these new laws (modifying their arrangement further over the following years), totaling 48. Whilst there were fears that people would be dissuaded from sea travel as a result of *Titanic's* loss, *Lusitania* attracted many passengers; many often changed travel arrangements to sail with her.

With the significance of sea power in British culture, and the fact that *Lusitania* and *Mauretania* were the fastest liners, they attracted great interest and publicity – practically being known as flagships for Britain. Until 1915 '*Lusy*' and '*Maurey*' had highly successful careers sailing between Liverpool and New York, and they were affectionately known as the 'Queens of the Atlantic'.

But in 1913 First Lord of the Admiralty Winston Churchill had requested *Lusitania* be prepared for naval conversion – primarily having six-inch gun mounts fitted as in her blueprints. Although conducted in secret, and the mounts disguised under coils of rope when she returned to Cunard, the Press soon revealed the true reason for the 'refit'. The guns themselves were never fitted.

Period postcard of *Lusitania* at sea.
Author's collection

Subsequently, on 16th March 1914 Churchill announced that 40 ships had been refitted for naval duties. But upon examination by naval architects in August 1914, serious doubts were raised concerning *Lusitania* and *Mauretania*. It was being increasingly thought that 'Armed Merchant Cruisers' were actually of minimal use, having limited firepower and no armour. Additionally, *Lusitania's* revolutionary turbines consumed vast quantities of coal – more than the Admiralty could justify. Therefore, both ships were returned again to Cunard and their arming order was cancelled.

With the advent of war, fewer people were crossing the Atlantic, and *Maure-tania* was laid up in Liverpool before later becoming a troop transport and hospital ship. *Lusitania*, repainted grey, conversely continued her transatlantic service at a reduced monthly rate, with boiler room four shut down to conserve coal. By May 1915 she had completed 201 crossings.

Back at the Admiralty, retired Admiral John 'Jackie' Fisher began to raise new concerns regarding requisitioning of civilian vessels, warning that:

> '…the recent arming of our British merchant ships is unfortunate, for it gives a hostile submarine an excellent excuse (if she needs one) for sinking them…'

Similarly, author Arthur Conan Doyle wrote a series of cautionary short war stories; one entitled *'Danger!'* centring on submarines as aggressors. Coincidentally, the famed liner torpedoed in the story was RMS *Olympic*, sister of the ill-fated *Titanic*…

In the earliest days of the war, however, submarines were generally not perceived as any real threat. But as men were beginning to get bogged down on the Western Front, the North Sea Fleet was ordered to make a quick-strike victory over Germany in the form of a large-scale sea blockade. Preventing any provisions from entering Germany, the resulting famine forced GrössAdmiral Tirpitz to act: with the German Imperial Fleet smaller than the British Grand Fleet, he instead used submarines to bypass the blockade, and British waters were declared a war zone in which all enemy ships were targets. As historians now recognise, this use of submarines against civilian vessels only began because of British naval action starving the German population; the U-boat was the sole method of retaliation.

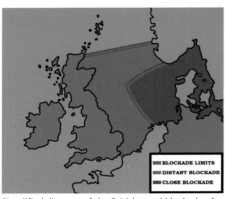

Simplified diagram of the British naval blockade of Germany. *Author*

Nonetheless, most U-boat captains followed a protocol called 'Cruiser Rules'. Signed under the Hague Conventions, these intended to allow neutral nations to continue trading in safety. Under the rules, all merchantmen – enemy or neutral – should stop and be searched if requested by a naval vessel. If war materials were found, the vessel would either be destroyed or confiscated at the naval commander's discretion. Should they choose to sink it, the safety of the crew was to be ensured, evacuating all aboard before any actual 'attack'. In 1914, Fisher had queried how submarines could adhere to the rules, as they had no provision for physically capturing a vessel nor for taking prisoners, asking:

'What if the Germans were to use submarines against commerce without restriction?'

Churchill replied:

'There are a few points on which I am not convinced. Of these, the greatest is the question of the use of submarines to sink merchant vessels. I do not believe this would ever be done by a civilised power.'

In order to signal and stop vessels for inspection, submarines stayed surfaced and often near-stationary, a fact that Churchill quickly realised. Intending to

capitalize on it, he providing top secret instructions to all merchant captains:
- British ships were, if necessary, to fly neutral nations' flags.
- If challenged, captains were to ram a hostile submarine at top speed to sink it.

He also ordered the construction of 'Q-Ships': armed cruisers disguised as merchantmen. Specifically designed to sink submarines, these blatantly violated the Hague Conventions. Losing 11 U-boats before realising what was happening, Germany thereafter considered any captain caught following these orders to be a spy, and in the case of Captain Fryatt and the SS *Brussels*, he was executed on capture. In spite of international concerns, primarily from America,

Germany publicly declared a counter-policy of 'unrestricted submarine warfare' – all enemy ships were to be sunk on sight without warning.

On 1st May 1915 *Lusitania* was scheduled to make her 202nd Atlantic crossing, eastbound from New York. Count Johann Von Bernstorff, the German ambassador to Washington, feared possible outrage should a U-boat attack any liner – particularly after a recent incident when the liner *Falaba*

Period postcard of *Lusitania* moored in New York.
Dan Smith collection

refused to obey 'Cruiser Rules' and was sunk with fatalities, including one American citizen. As a result, he placed a warning in newspapers concerning the risk of attack by the advert for the sailing of the next major British vessel – *Lusitania*:

'Notice!
Travellers intending to embark on the Atlantic voyage are reminded that a state
of war exists between Germany and her allies and Great Britain and her allies;
that the zone of war includes the waters adjacent to the British Isles; that, in
accordance with formal notice given by the Imperial German Government,
vessels flying the flag of Great Britain, or any of her allies, are liable to
destruction in those waters and that travellers sailing in the war zone on ships
of Great Britain or her allies do so at their own risk.'

In spite of this warning, not only was there no concern but *Lusitania* departed with the largest complement of passengers since the start of the war: 1959 passengers and crew. The most notable passengers were theatrical producer Charles Frohman and millionaire Alfred Vanderbilt. Both ignored the warning; Vanderbilt saw it as a 'joke in poor taste', believing in his own good luck (Alfred's 'luck', though, being often erroneously confused with his uncle, George Vanderbilt, who had previously cancelled a passage on *Titanic*). They were not alone in their views – survivor Desmond Cox noting:

'There were lots of warnings, and people just didn't take them seriously.'

Arguably the main reasons for this complacency were the belief that *Lusitania's* 'natural defences' – her speed and size – protected her, and President Wilson's claims that Americans, as neutrals, had unrestricted access to travel anywhere in spite of unrestricted submarine warfare.

The last photograph of *Lusitania*.
Eric Sauder Collection

However, *Lusitania* had already narrowly avoided submarines on previous voyages and, more pressingly, passengers were unaware of part of her cargo. Loaded with approximately 4200 crates of Remmington rifle case cartridges and 1271 cases of non-explosive fuses and shrapnel shells, amongst others, these were omitted from her manifest until an incomplete supplementary manifest was issued on 5th May – four days after departure. Furthermore, it has been claimed that several cases listed as 'cheese', 'butter', 'lard' and 'bacon' were placed in non-refrigerated holds – some believing them to have potentially contained illegal high explosives. Whether true or not, *Lusitania* contained munitions: far from a purely 'civilian' vessel, this contraband made her a legitimate target…

In command was Captain William Tuner, who held the position from March 1915 and had previously commanded her from 1908-9. With an unblemished record and forty years' experience, Turner was recognised as an experienced and efficient mariner. Conversely, he strongly disliked passengers and avoided them whenever possible. Ironically this made him very popular! Cunard duly appointed Captain John Anderson as staff captain, primarily in charge of the crew but unofficially to deal with the social aspects of command. As for the crew, morale was especially low – to the extent that many crewmembers deserted in New York; replacements being unfamiliar with the ship.

Arguably, though, Turner had one principal problem – a very laid-back attitude, being utterly set in his ways. On 30th April 1915 he was an expert witness for the *'Titanic* Liability Hearings' in New York. When asked if anything had been learnt, he replied:

'Not the slightest; it will happen again.'

At 12:30pm the next day, 1st May, he and *Lusitania* sailed to Liverpool on her regular course. On the 6th he received the first of numerous Admiralty messages: 'Submarines active off South Coast of Ireland'. A general announcement was repeated to *Lusitania* that evening, stating:

'Pass harbours at full speed; steer mid-channel course. Submarines off Fastnet.'

While some passengers showed concern, Turner listed the aforementioned 'natural defences' when declining requests for a lifeboat drill. However, upon nearing the war zone he pre-emptively ordered all lifeboats swung out, a partial blackout of the ship and watertight doors closed (excluding coal bunkers, required for the operation of the ship). At the passengers' concert he informed them that, weather permitting, they were to sail at full steam to reach Liverpool for the afternoon high tide.

Lusitania's Bridge. *Eric Sauder Collection*

But the weather deteriorated. The morning of 7th May was very foggy and speed was reduced to 15 knots, while the number of lookouts on the bridge and foc'sle (the forward-most deck at the bow) was increased. At 11:25am another Admiralty message was issued, *Lusitania* receiving it at 1:00pm:

'Submarines active in southern part of Irish Channel, last heard of 20 miles south of Coningbeg Light Vessel; make certain Lusitania *gets this.'*

A further message noted:

'Submarines five miles south of Cape Clear, proceeding west when sighted at 10am'.

This was received at 1:00pm, with *Lusitania* 20 miles east of Cape Clear. While the instructions given to Turner have been much discussed, it is certain he was never informed of any prior attacks or sinkings on his intended course. According to some, Turner even expected the voyage to be delayed or cancelled before departing New York. There have also been debates over whether Turner received orders to change course and sail to Queenstown – something the Admiralty denied, while Turner later stated he believed a coded message dictating this was received. Unfortunately, the Queenstown Admiralty signal records are now missing.

Entering the war zone, Turner should have followed official Admiralty directives:
- Steer a mid-channel course.
- Avoid headlands.
- Sail at full speed.
- Sail a zig-zag course.

Period postcard of *Lusitania* and *Mauretania* (depicted). *David Lean collection*

Happier times: Period postcard of *Lusitania* moored in Liverpool. *David Lean collection*

Even if the Admiralty had omitted any of these instructions on this crossing, with the fog mostly burnt away Turner should have remembered them from earlier voyages and acted upon them. Strictly speaking, there was no 'channel' in that area to follow and *Lusitania* was farther away from the headlands than on previous voyages, but conversely it has never been satisfactorily explained why on this voyage he failed to follow the latter points on speed and course. However, it is reasonable to assume he was slightly disorientated, as these orders are exceedingly dangerous without knowing the vessel's exact position – difficult in fog. This is further supported by his final crucial action: ordering a four-point bearing. This proves uncertainty about their position, while the earlier message indicating submarines 20 miles astern gave a false sense of security.

With the Irish coast in sight, passengers believed danger was passed; one saying 'Thank God for a safe journey – we can see Ireland now'. In order to take the bearing it was needed to sail parallel with the coast, and at 1:40pm Turner ordered a turn to starboard.

Well before *Lusitania* had left New York, another voyage had begun that would converge at this very moment. Sailing on 30th April, four U-boats left Emden bound for Liverpool, two under the orders:

'Large English troop transports expected starting from Liverpool, Bristol Channel, Dartmouth. In order to do considerable damage to transports, U-20 and U-27 are to be dispatched as soon as possible. Distribute stations there. Get to stations on the fastest possible route.'

Launched at the Kaiserliche Werft shipyard in Danzig on 18th December 1912, the Unterseeboot *U-20* had been commissioned on 5th August 1913 into the Kaiserliche Marine III Flottille. One of four 'U-19' Class submarines, she was 210 feet long, 20 feet wide and had a top surface speed of 15.4 knots; 9.5 when submerged. With a crew of 35, this Class was the first German type with diesel engines. Originally an advanced design, by 1915 she was beginning to be somewhat outdated. Intended to be her primary weapon under 'Cruiser Rules' was an 88mm calibre deck gun, and she sported four 20-inch calibre torpedo tubes: two forward, two aft. The common G-6 type torpedo used was highly unreliable, having a habit of either changing course or for the 'safety' (protecting the detonator) failing to release. *U-20's* second commander was Kapitänleutnant Walther Schwieger. He was a highly respected U-boat commander, having joined the Kaiserliche Marine in 1903 and previously captaining *U-14* before being transferred in December 1914. By March 1915 *U-20* had sunk six British ships off the south Irish coast, all under Schwieger, totalling approximately 21,000 tons.

This voyage Schwieger followed a course around Scotland and West Ireland, *U-20* reaching Fastnet on 5th May. At 5:50pm that day they halted the unarmed schooner *Earl of Latham* off Kinsale, obeying 'Cruiser Rules'. After being searched and evacuated, she was sunk using the deck gun. On 6th May two steamers were sunk off the Coningbeg lightship, although numerous vessels had previously escaped in the fog. Nonetheless, crew morale was especially high. Returning to the South Irish coastline owing to limited fuel, on 7th May *U-20* sighted an elderly British cruiser heading towards Queenstown. Now believed to be HMS *Juno*, its departure removed the primary naval protection in the area that Turner appears to have been expecting – essentially leaving *Lusitania* undefended. Significantly, the Admiralty had decoded virtually all transmissions sent from *U-20*, and already knew of *U-20*, its movements and its victims. Aside from the vague messages to

On sea trials. *Eric Sauder Collection*

Lusitania, though, particularly that referring to the Coningbeg Light Vessel, the Admiralty failed to relay any detailed information or warning to Turner.

Low on provisions, fuel and torpedoes, Schwieger decided to return home at 10:00am 7th May after a successful patrol. Having surfaced due to the fog, at 1:20pm Schwieger sighted a steamer:

'*2:20 pm:*

Ahead and to starboard four funnels and two masts of a steamer with course perpendicular to us come into sight (coming from SSW it steered towards Galley Head). Ship is made out to be a large passenger steamer.

2:25pm:

Submerged to a depth of 11 metres and went ahead at full speed, taking a course converging with the one of the steamer, hoping it might change its course to starboard along the Irish coast.

2:35pm:

The steamer turns to starboard, takes course to Queenstown, thus making possible an approach for a shot. Until 3:00pm we ran at high speed in order to gain position directly ahead.

3:10pm:

Clean bow shot at a distance of 700 metres (G-torpedo, 3 metres depth adjustment), angle 90°, estimated speed 22 knots. Torpedo hits starboard side right behind the Bridge.'

The log was written to German time – the torpedo was fired just after 2:10pm GMT. Purportedly, *U-20* crewmember Charles Voegele objected to attacking a passenger ship, but was ignored – the attack going ahead. However, the omission of any reference to such a 'mutiny' in any official documents or crew memoirs strongly suggests the story was a later fabrication to deflect some of the propaganda damage done to Germany. While prior British Admiralty

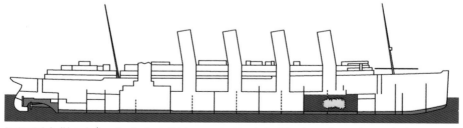

Lusitania's bulkheads (longitudinal subdivisions marked by dashed lines), uptakes and torpedo damage.
Author

discussions, querying what impact *Lusitania's* theoretical sinking might have, insinuate that the fallibility of her bulkhead design was recognised within the Admiralty it is commonly agreed that Schwieger did not expect to do any serious damage. Firing an unreliable G-6 torpedo, it was questionable whether it would even detonate. At best, he may score a moral victory by denting the reputation of one of Britain's finest vessels. Ironically, it was only due to Turner's final turn to starboard that Scheiger even had a chance to fire. It was claimed that Pilot Lanz only actually identified *Lusitania* after the torpedo struck. Likely a later attempt at deflecting blame, the limited number of four-funnel liners and the undoubted desire of all U-boat commanders to encounter *Lusitania* makes this unlikely.

Lookout Leslie Morton first sighted the torpedo off *Lusitania's* starboard bow. According to survivor Desmond Cox:

'When the torpedo hit, dishes were flying all over and people were actually knocked out of their chairs.'

While the exact location where the torpedo struck is unknown, partly due to later fabrications about a 'second torpedo', most accounts place it across the first two starboard bunkers. Large amounts of coal found around the wreck further support this. However, Peskett's calculations suggest that with the bunker doors closed, she should merely list 15 degrees. But Schwieger's torpedo instead started a chain reaction that still remains highly contested. A few seconds after the impact, a second more powerful explosion occurred, shaking the entire vessel and sending a column of water high into the air, destroying deck vents and carrying away a lifeboat. It was this second mystery blast that sank *Lusitania*. As Schwieger noted:

'The explosion of the torpedo must have been followed by a second one (boiler or coal or powder?).'

So what caused it? Ironically it is now believed the Admiralty feared that the munitions cargo had exploded, so encouraged rumours of a 'second torpedo' – emphasising German aggression while also deflecting blame from themselves. This was, though, a complete fiction. Studies of *Lusitania's* wreck show that the munitions (stowed under the foremast) did not detonate – some have even being recovered. Therefore, while significant in terms of moral legitimacy, *Lusitania's* cargo can be conclusively relegated to a footnote when considering the actual sinking.

Instead, the most likely theories are either a coal dust explosion or a boiler failure – the torpedo triggering this second fatal explosion. Both have been frequently argued, but the complete loss of power at 2:14pm – barely four minutes after the torpedo struck – indicates steam pressure must have drastically dropped. This is further supported by the subsequent loss of electrical power a minute later – the dynamos only generating through centripetal force as they slowed. Experiments have refuted the likelihood of coal dust being in the right conditions to explode, and this rapid loss of pressure supports the case for a major failure in her steam machinery – a boiler or steam pipe explosion the most probable cause. Each boiler room had an independent steam pipe connecting it and the engines, however, these pipes converged into one before the engine room – and before the master isolation valves. With the individual boiler cut-off valves open, as needed to power the engines, then any failed or severed pipe would cause all the other boiler rooms to vent pressure back to the broken section, rapidly emptying the boilers of steam.

As for how a torpedo could trigger such an explosive steam failure, the near-empty longitudinal bunkers on the starboard side would have filled almost instantly after the torpedo (dousing down the coal dust), but the small bunker doors would have limited the initial inrush of water into the boiler room itself. The increasing pressure of water against this undoubtedly-damaged bulkhead would have very rapidly led to a sudden rise in flooding – flash-cooling the steam machinery. This sudden temperature change would have triggered thermal shock in the metal, cracking it, and the escaping steam pressure would thus cause a massive steam explosion – the fatal second blast.

Sailing at approximately 18 knots, *Lusitania* was moving too fast to safely lower the lifeboats and her forward momentum forced more water into her hull. As she increasingly listed, many open portholes rapidly submerged – negating virtually all the watertight compartments. With no power or steering Turner could not check speed, so ordered filled lifeboats to wait before lowering. The Marconi wireless set had an emergency dynamo, and was able to send three brief messages:

> *'SOS We think we are off Kinsale.'*
> *'Position ten miles off Kinsale come at once, big list.'*
> *'Please come with all haste.'*

Period Anglo-French postcard commemorating the sinking. *Author's collection*

After ten minutes the foc'sle was awash, with many crewmembers trapped in the submerged bow. The ensuing evacuation was a shambles. *Lusitania* was sinking so rapidly that there was no time for evacuation procedures, and orders to the crew were difficult to hear above the turmoil on deck. The list, by now exceeding 30 degrees, made the port side lifeboats unusable – swinging inboard, they crushed people on the deck. Of the few port boats pushed out and lowered, they were so damaged after striking protrusions on the hull that they threatened to sink. Conversely, the starboard side lifeboats swung out over seven feet away from the deck, so were increasingly difficult to fill and lower. With passengers panicking and a depleted crew unused to lowering lifeboats, many capsized or were upended spilling occupants into the sea. Some were lowered too quickly after each other, crushing lifeboats already in the water. A number of canvas-sided 'collapsible' lifeboats were found to have been fixed to the deck with layers of paint, metal parts rusted solid, making them useless. In total, one port side lifeboat and five starboard side lifeboats were successfully lowered – only six out of 48. Alfred Vanderbilt was last seen helping women put on lifejackets while Charles Frohman was last heard

Arguably the most famed Lusitania recuitment poster, depicting the horror of the sinking.
Senan Molony collection

reciting lines from 'Peter Pan'. Turner intended to go down with his ship, but was knocked unconscious and clear when the Bridge submerged.

Partially righting herself, *Lusitania* sank at 2:28pm, eighteen minutes after the torpedo struck. Watching from the cliffs at the Old Head of Kinsale, young George Henderson's family picnic had become terrified witness to the full spectacle:

'*She'd reached the stage where even the propellers were out of the water, which weren't going round – you could see them there, and then, as if on a slide she just disappeared underneath the waves.*'

Through his periscope Schwieger also witnessed the sinking in horror:
'*3:25pm:
Since it seems as if the steamer will keep above water only a short time, we dived to a depth of 24 metres and ran out to sea. It would have been impossible for me, anyhow, to fire a second torpedo into this crowd of people struggling to save their lives.*'

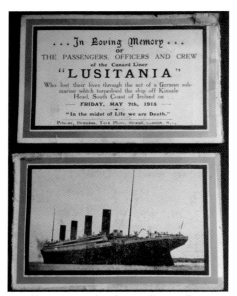

Period 'In Memoriam' card, ironically actually depicting RMS *Titanic*. *Nikki Allen collection*

Lusitania's distress calls were received by the Queenstown Admiralty station and a flotilla of 12 fishing craft and naval patrol vessels proceeded to the scene as fast as they could, arriving two hours later. Of 1959 people on board only 764 survived, including Turner. 1195 had perished. Later vessels recovered some bodies, Cunard offering monetary incentives, but most victims were never recovered.

The authorities were quick to react in the aftermath of the disaster. Opening on 9th May 1915, Queenstown held a Coroner's Inquiry to identify the cause of death of five victims. Described as 'prolonged immersion and exhaustion in the sea', this was labelled by the jury as a 'crime of wilful and wholesale murder.' The Inquest looked in comparative detail at the circumstances surrounding the attack, with Captain Turner as a prominent witness. Questioned over speed, lack of warning (about other sinkings or *U-20's* precise position) and precautions taken – Turner often explaining he was not at liberty to divulge Admiralty messages – the Coroner concluded by expressing sympathy and crediting his courage.

With international horror at what was seen as an 'act of premeditated barbaric savagery', the initial warning in American newspapers made for ideal British propaganda. Newspaper coverage of the mass funerals and the Inquiry furthering the 'pirate Hun' view, Press accounts becoming ever-more inaccurate. In America the attack was immediately condemned by President Wilson and citizens alike – Theodore Roosevelt even went so far as to call it:

'Piracy on a vaster scale than any old time pirate ever practiced.'

Schwieger and *U-20* returned home initially amid congratulation, but he was soon heavily criticised for placing Germany in a bad situation by upsetting neutral America. While Germany claimed *Lusitania* as a valid target, recounting her naval intentions, worldwide anti-German riots and American calls to end unrestricted submarine warfare demonstrated international opinion. Labelled a war criminal in Britain, Schwieger later received the 'Pour le Mérite' award (also known as the 'Blue Max') for one of the highest combined tonnages sunk,

964 W   CUNARD LINER, " LUSITANIA."   BEAGLES' POSTCARDS
THIS MAMMOTH ATLANTIC LINER, WITH 2,160 PASSENGERS, OFFICERS AND CREW WAS, WITHOUT WARNING, TORPEDOED AND SUNK BY A GERMAN SUBMARINE ON MAY 7TH, 1915, EIGHT MILES OFF THE OLD HEAD OF KINSALE, IRELAND. 1,399 INNOCENT LIVES WERE UNHAPPILY SACRIFICED THROUGH THIS MOST HORRIBLE AND INDEFENSIBLE ACT OF PREMEDITATED, BARBARIC SAVAGERY.

Period postcard commemorating the sinking (note the critical propaganda in the caption). *Author's collection*

being the sixth most successful U-boat captain of the war. This tonnage did not include *Lusitania*.

One of the most significant pieces of British Great War propaganda strangely originated in Germany. Sculptor Karl Goetz manufactured many medallions throughout the war, and produced one commemorating the sinking and the arrogance of Britain and Cunard. Featuring guns and an aircraft on *Lusitania's* decks, Death selling tickets while warning Germans are ignored, and the comments 'No Contraband' and 'Business above all', the medal also included an incorrect pre-sinking date – purportedly from an inaccurate German newspaper report. Limited in production, and despite a corrected version being produced, one of the earlier medals fell into British hands. Claiming the date as proof of premeditation, Selfridges department store released 300,000 copies for sale to demonstrate the so-dubbed 'German Naval Victory'. With the sinking leading to mass rioting against

Reverse of the 'Lusitania Medal'. *Author's collection*

German shops and businesses, the propaganda value of these replicas was immense, helping redouble the enthusiasm of the public towards the war. Through a strange irony, the depiction of *Lusitania* sinking – grossly erroneous, sinking stern first and with a ram bow – is actually a simplified rendition of HMS *Aboukir* sinking during the 'Cressy Fiasco', taken from another popular contemporary medallion.

Reverse of the Ziegler 'Weddigen Medal' (left) and obverse of the Goetz 'Lusitania Medal' (right) showing the duplication of the sinking ship image. *Author's collection*

On 15th June 1915 the official Board of Trade Inquiry was opened in Westminster under Admiralty Wreck Commissioner Lord Mersey, the man who chaired the British *Titanic* Inquiry. Lasting five days, it was a complete whitewash intending to deflect criticism, act as propaganda and mask the fact that munitions had been on board. The Admiralty was very selective with witnesses, even suggesting to some that recalling two or more torpedoes would be 'helpful', and the manner which Mersey and Attorney-General Sir Edward Carson examined witnesses was highly discriminatory. For example, when witnesses began to give too much information Lord Mersey would cut them off. This was particularly the case when referring to her bulkheads.

Furthermore, the Admiralty almost made Turner a scapegoat. To this effect, a memorandum by Captain Webb of the Admiralty Trade Division (on behalf of the Admiralty) stated:

'On the facts at present disclosed the Master appears to have displayed an almost inconceivable negligence, or that he has been got at by the Germans.'

A full Admiralty investigation revealed no German links; the emphasis turning to incompetence or negligence, which Mersey found himself being strongly suggested so to find. With criticisms by Churchill in Parliament, confusing examination by Carson on irrelevant or (in the case of zig-zagging) potentially fictitious orders, and a lack of questioning of the Admiralty's actions leading up to the sinking, Turner's reputation was seriously damaged. For what could have been a clear-cut case of simply blaming 'the enemy', this is very peculiar. While effectively succumbing to Admiralty pressure concerning the number of torpedoes and even crediting the Admiralty for the diligence with which they forewarned *Lusitania*, Mersey, however, steadfastly supported Turner and recognised his preventative actions. He went so far as to state that even if all 'advice' (not being specifically compulsory) had been carried out, it was doubtful that disaster would have been averted:

'His omission to follow the advice in all respects cannot fairly be attributed either to negligence or incompetence. He exercised his judgement for the best.

It was the judgement of a skilled and experienced man, and although others might have acted differently and perhaps more successfully he ought not, in my opinion, to be blamed.'

This finding shocked many survivors, and some historians still question Turner's actions, although it did provide a rich source of propaganda and international discussion over unrestricted submarine warfare. These discussions culminated in the *'Lusitania* letters' by President Wilson and the resignation of the American Secretary of State, William Bryan. Along with 'two' torpedoes sinking her, conceal-

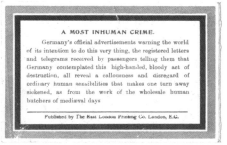

Extract from a period 'In Memoriam' card criticising the German newspaper warning. *Author's collection*

ing the mystery second explosion, the Inquiry covered up Admiralty messages, open portholes and even omitted several accounts of lifeboats leaking through age – instead blaming this on damage during lowering. While her bulkheads were fleetingly referenced in the final report, no mention of design defects was made, and the sole witness who claimed munitions had detonated was actively discredited. In spite of these many and varied factors it was decreed that Germany was the sole culprit. Arguably the best demonstration of how dubious the Inquiry was were Mersey's actions immediately afterwards: waiving his fee and resigning from his post. As he later recounted:

'It was a damned dirty business.'

As the war progressed, *Lusitania* became truly infamous: the ensuing propaganda campaigns temporarily ended unrestricted submarine warfare, and ultimately helped turn American opinion in favour of entering the war. While

A
German Naval Victory

"With joyful pride we contemplate this latest deed of our navy. . . .'—
Kölnische Volkszeitung, 10th May, 1915.

This medal has been struck in Germany with the object of keeping alive in German hearts the recollection of the glorious achievement of the German Navy in deliberately destroying an unarmed passenger ship, together with 1,198 non-combatants, men, women and children.

On the obverse, under the legend "No contraband" *(Keine Bannware),* there is a representation of the *Lusitania* sinking. The designer has put in guns and aeroplanes, which (as was certified by United States Government officials after inspection) the *Lusitania* did *not* carry ; but has conveniently omitted to put in the women and children, which the world knows she *did* carry.

On the reverse, under the legend "Business above all" *(Geschäft über alles),* the figure of Death sits at the booking office of the Cunard Line and gives out tickets to passengers, who refuse to attend to the warning against submarines given by a German. This picture seeks apparently to propound the theory that if a murderer warns his victim of his intention, the guilt of the crime will rest with the victim, not with the murderer.

Propaganda leaflet issued with the Selfridges copies of the 'Lusitania Medal'. *(Author's collection)*

not the official reason for doing so, only actually occurring some two years later, their soldiers were frequently heard to shout *'Lusitania!'* when advancing into battle. Once peace was declared memorials were erected and, through continued publicity, she remains still well known today.

Retracing back to the attack itself, what were the factors that led to this calamity? The torpedoing of any ship depends on numerous factors – the skill of the submarine commander is but one. While Schwieger had great ability, four broad potential reasons are apparent to consider: coincidence (and unexpected consequences), failure of duty (as in negligence), miscalculation (basing actions on incomplete information) and conspiracy. This last has been much debated over *Lusitania*, especially due to its far-reaching political and propaganda consequences.

Arguably the first issue is the legitimacy of the attack itself. It has been conclusively proved that *Lusitania* was carrying armaments, so although carrying neutral and civilian passengers and not acting as an 'Armed Merchant Cruiser', she was nonetheless a legitimate target. Had Schwieger followed Cruiser Rules and attempted to stop her, Turner probably would have adopted Churchill's

Memorial at Cobh on the centenary of the sinking. *Nikki Allen*

illegal orders to permit escape. The moral implications, however, are less clear-cut. Schwieger would have realised the presence of passengers, but it would have been logical to expect *Lusitania* to sink slowly enough to be successfully evacuated. Lastly, it is now recognised that he did not 'lie in wait' for *Lusitania* as the British accused, with subsequent propaganda influencing public perception of his legitimate actions.

Coincidence as a factor was highly significant. Long before *Lusitania* even departed, the British blockade of Germany and Churchill's covert orders led firstly to submarine attacks, then to the use of unrestricted submarine warfare. Judging by Churchill's comment on 'civilised nations' not attacking merchant vessels, and the lack of support for Fisher's warnings, it appears unlikely that the Admiralty expected Germany to adopt this equally-illegal tactic. Furthermore, pre-war publicity highlighting *Lusitania's* speed and size not only gave a false sense of security but arguably led Schwieger to expect his torpedo would do little damage, particularly as G-6 torpedoes were notoriously unreliable. On the day itself, foggy weather resulted in reducing speed and probably resulted in Turner's call for a four-point bearing – their position being unclear. This, coupled to the coincidence of *U-20* being present to sight his quarry, led to *Lusitania* coming into range. As for the actual sinking, the second explosion was completely unexpected and the fact that its cause is still debated means her design cannot necessarily be held accountable. Whatever the cause, the knock-on effects of the explosion and associated loss of steam pressure led to some watertight doors remaining open and prevented any attempts to slow down sufficiently to launch the lifeboats while still relatively upright.

Lusitania departing New York. *David Lean collection*

Just as significant as coincidence is the presence of potential errors. The known defects in *Lusitania's* bulkheads and overall height played a significant role in the sinking – her dangerous instability worsening the effects of the flooding and preventing lifeboats from being successfully lowered (as unwittingly predicted by Wilding in 1912). While Peskett and the designers would appear to be culpable, they were working within strict limits placed by the Admiralty: calling for longitudinal bulkheads and the narrow width. Turner's attitude, linked to a false sense of security through *Lusitania's* size and speed, is another factor. While some precautions were made, the lack of any lifeboat drill prevented passengers knowing where to go, although admittedly the speed of the sinking would have rendered any organised plan useless. Lifeboat launching – difficult due to the list – was worsened by the new crew being unfamiliar with how to lower them. However, Turner's failure to follow Admiralty orders (particularly zig-zagging) leads to the greatest debate.

Turner never admitted that the fog may have caused him to lose his positioning, Admiralty orders thus being dangerous when close to the shore. Possibly believing in *Lusitania's* 'natural defences', the Admiralty message insinuating that they were beyond all submarines, or just simply being set in his ways, he clearly was not expecting to be attacked. This attitude in a war zone where submarines were known to operate could well be considered negligent, but it also explains ordering the four-point bearing – lost in fog, it was a rational action if believing there was no submarine threat nearby. But this suggests a marked difference between 'negligence' and mere miscalculation. While Turner's actions ultimately led to the sinking, were they culpable or conversely based on incomplete or erroneous information?

Turner probably should have had more reservations sailing in a war zone, plainly being overconfident, but he did order some precautions, indicating he was not as blasé as his detractors claimed. The significance of his actions hinge on the instructions and warnings sent to him by the Admiralty, which were at best poor. No messages concerning previous sinkings were sent to *Lusitania*, and the few messages concerning submarines that were sent indicated she was travelling in the opposite direction and had already safely passed them. Had this perspective been correct then Turner would have had little to fear, and the Admiralty's measures would only have slowed them down. In a private conversation with Third Officer Bestic in 1932, Turner admitted having 'false confidence' due to the messages received, also criticising the Admiralty and Churchill not only for publically implying his negligence but because 'they didn't even explain to me about zig-zagging'. He added that detailed Admiralty messages were only adopted in 1917. Particularly when considering that no escort was provided, although it had been on earlier voyages, it seems likely that the Admiralty rather than Turner was negligent in its actions – potentially explaining why Lord Mersey fully exonerated him.

There is one final potential factor – deliberate conspiracy by the Admiralty. Sabotage is easily the most contentious *Lusitania* debate, with Churchill credited as the 'mastermind'. The poor Admiralty messages to Turner (plus accusations that some were never sent), along with providing no warning of the other sinkings has been used to suggest that the Admiralty purposely let *Lusitania* sail into known danger, compounded by orders to remove HMS *Juno* from the area – the only significant naval presence. This also ties in with their accusations of Turner; conspirators claiming him to be a 'scapegoat'. The Admiralty certainly knew of *U-20's* location but failed to inform Turner, and their role in silencing claims of munitions on board during the Inquiry is generally accepted as a cover-up – the question being whether covering up earlier Admiralty negligence or planned destruction. Concerning Churchill's involvement, three months beforehand he wrote in a letter dated 12th February 1915:

> *'It is most important to attract neutral shipping to our shores, in the hope especially of embroiling the U.S. with Germany.' 'For our part, we want the traffic – the more the better and if some of it gets into trouble, better still.'*

Furthermore, in a 1937 edition of the *News of the World*, Churchill stated:

> *'In spite of all its horror, we must regard the sinking of the Lusitania as an event most important and favourable to the Allies... The poor babies who perished in the ocean struck a blow at German power more deadly than could have been achieved by the sacrifice of a hundred thousand fighting men.'*

But that said, there is a major difference between seeing the ramifications of a potential event and actively engineering it – there being no concrete proof for the latter. Even if he did hope for *Lusitania* to be embroiled, importantly Churchill – as with most people – probably believed in *Lusitania's* publicised safety. Conversely, the elderly HMS *Juno* was thought susceptible to torpedoes

The "Lusitania" (German) Medal

An exact replica of the medal which was designed in Germany and distributed to commemorate the sinking of the "Lusitania."

This indicates the true feeling the War Lords endeavour to stimulate, and is proof positive that such crimes are not merely regarded favourably, but are given every encouragement in the land of Kultur.

The "Lusitania" was sunk by a German submarine on May 7th, 1915. She had on board at the time 1,951 passengers and crew, of whom 1,198 perished.

The 'Lusitania Medal' in its box with description.
Author's collection

and potentially at risk, explaining her removal in preference over that of the faster and 'safer' *Lusitania*. As the Admiralty had influenced *Lusitania's* design and clearly knew of the resultant risk – the same as with HMS *Juno* – their failure to protect her was inexcusable. But increasingly pressured throughout the war, concentrating on their own ships rather than a rejected civilian 'Armed Merchant Cruiser' and gradually believing publicity over *Lusitania's* safety, the Admiralty simply forgot about the danger. Therefore, in all probability the actions described that fit such a conspiracy were more likely the result of subsequent 'damage control' minimising embarrassing Admiralty failings, rather than any grand scheme. They were substantially to blame, but only through negligence rather than active design.

The factors of coincidence, negligence, miscalculation and conspiracy were all prominent, but they have varying significance. Coincidence led to Schwieger sighting his victim, and in any event it was the unexpected second explosion that ultimately sank her. However, with humanity's desire to allocate blame for losses, negligence and miscalculation became significant in explaining how that final set of coincidences came about. Miscalculations had a direct impact on this, yet these decisions were well intended. It was only after the tragedy that subsequent conspiracy theories (or more accurately, 'damage control') complicated the story in a bid to hide perceived failings and negligence that left her vulnerable.

The loss of RMS *Lusitania* may not have triggered American involvement in World War One, but it still had a major impact. The publicity it gave to unrestricted submarine warfare led to a propaganda coup – the sinking being recognised as the first large-scale civilian loss to garner such widespread public attention. It ultimately demonstrated that in modern warfare *everyone* was at risk.

But the responsibility for the loss does not lie solely with Schwieger – many principal factors stem from action (and inaction) by the British Admiralty. This was not a planned conspiracy – even with Churchill once referring pre-war to *Lusitania* as 'livebait' (comparable to the *Cressy* 'Livebait Squadron'). Instead, the Admiralty's restrictive specifications for her design, along with numerous failings immediately prior to the sinking were more probably the result of unintended negligence, ultimately leading to her vulnerability. While making some errors, Turner appears mostly free from blame – his actions were logical based on the (poor) warnings given. Peskett realised the dangers of the design, however, he was constrained by Admiralty orders. The significance to the disaster of her inherently unsafe bulkhead layout is paramount – as Turner regularly said when describing his failing health in old age:

'I am all right fore and aft, but my longitudinal bulkhead's given way.'

Period postcard of *Lusitania* at speed. *David Lean collection*

Cunard deserves some blame for transporting munitions, although again this was primarily the fault of the Admiralty and the War Office. Conversely, coincidence led to Schwieger finding *Lusitania*, and the weather forcing her speed down. The consequences of these were significant, but had it not been for Admiralty messages instilling false confidence in Turner, he would not have necessarily ordered the four-point bearing that placed him in Schwieger's cross-hairs.

Despite many being victims, *Lusitania's* passengers sadly also bear some responsibility. While having the option to sail on a truly neutral vessel, they decided to sail into a war zone on a belligerent ship in spite of warnings. The warnings do not excuse the attack, but they do prevent any claims of ignorance of the danger, even if believing the false security of *Lusitania's* supposed superiority. That the American authorities led people to think they could sail with impunity ultimately makes them and their isolationist stance accountable too, particularly concerning the propaganda significance of the 'innocents' lost aboard.

Much debate has been made over Churchill's personal involvement – whether he masterminded the supposed plot. If correct, then he was ultimately to blame. However, his actions in arming merchantmen, giving illegal orders and building Q-ships directly resulted in unrestricted submarine warfare. Consequently, *Lusitania* was attacked without warning. Although realistically only occurring by accident, Churchill directly helped orchestrate the disaster. As Fisher secretly wrote on 29th March 1916 to his friend GrössAdmiral Tirpitz:

'I don't blame you for the submarine business, I'd have done exactly the same myself.'

So how much was the sinking the result of 'almost inconceivable negligence'? Although Captain Webb's quote no longer applies solely to Turner – rather the body that originally said it – the torpedoing of *Lusitania* was the direct consequence of extraordinary levels of coincidence, negligence and a series of errors stemming from her very construction. Submarine commanders are generally held accountable for fatalities caused by their attacks, but nothing is so clearcut. People and events far removed can still play a major role, and fault regularly lies further afield, whether for the best or worst of intentions. To quote explorer Professor (formerly Doctor) Robert Ballard:

'When you have a disaster like this one, so many truly innocent people – and they were innocent; children, women, people from neutral countries and had absolutely nothing to do with the War, died, you always want to say well who's to blame – who can we pin this on? And from what I can see, everyone was to blame; it was not a grand performance on the part of the human race.'

Period postcard of *Lusitania* with an ironic 'hands across the sea' motto. *Author's collection*

'THE BRIDGE IS DOWN!'
The Tay Bridge Disaster

'Beautiful Railway Bridge of the Silv'ry Tay!
Alas! I am very sorry to say
That ninety lives have been taken away
On the last Sabbath day of 1879,
Which will be remember'd for a very long time.'

So opens William Topaz McGonagall's famous poem, one of three unwittingly presenting a chronology of Dundee's Victorian engineering history. Over 130 years have passed, but stories still abound of the most famous railway accident in British history – the Tay Bridge Disaster.

Subject to myth and mystery, much remains unknown, but a new theory offers for the first time the true origin of the disaster.

At the height of the Victorian 'Railway Age' there were over a hundred railway companies nationally. In Scotland the leading two were the Caledonian Railway and the North British Railway (NBR) – fierce rivals competing for traffic from London. By the 1850s the companies'

Period postcard showing the collapsed bridge.
Author's collection

lines had spread, but with two massive obstacles – the Firths of Tay and Forth. Dependent on ferries, these bottlenecks constricted traffic immeasurably. Enter Thomas Bouch. Born in 1822 he was an acclaimed engineer, having designed the first ever roll-on-roll-off train ferries for the Forth, built tramways and becoming particularly well-known for lattice-work bridges. His overall aim was to be the man to bridge the Tay and Forth. In 1854 and 1866 he proposed to the NBR a bridge across the Tay, ultimately from Wormit Bay on the south bank to Dundee itself to the north. On these occasions, however, the proposals were undone by finances and the Caledonian Railway objecting. Detractors called it the 'rainbow bridge'; this phrase backfired, encouraging support when proposed a third time in 1869. After continual debate, the Act for construction was finally passed on 15th July 1870.

The bridge's design had to overcome many challenges and changed virtually throughout construction. Of lattice form, it was to be the world's largest bridge at over 2 miles long. The Tay Navigation Committee, fearing the ports of Dundee and Perth would be blocked, had also opposed until Bouch promised his bridge would permit sailing vessels to pass even at high tide. To enable this the central portion of the bridge had to be 90 feet above the water, so while trains ran over the top of the majority of the bridge, in the centre they ran through the middle of what were called the 'High Girders'.

However, in the first of many issues the contractors changed after the original firm's head died. The second contractor's head went steadily insane and also died, so a third was contracted: Hopkin Gilkes and Company, which had financial difficulties and went bust shortly after completion. Then it was found the surveyors misjudged the riverbed. In the centre, right under the High Girders, there was no bedrock. Forced to redesign, Bouch had to create artificial foundations on which were placed cast iron piers clad in brick, rather than piers of solid brick and stone as intended. Further keeping weight down, the planned brick columns were each replaced with six latticed iron columns over 70 feet tall, the foundations of which were set into the piers by only 2.5 feet. The High Girders themselves were reduced in number to two of 227 feet long and 11 some 247 feet long – 13 in total. Through the needs of such ironwork to expand and contract, these were positioned on rollers and held in place by gravity – only three of 14 columns were actually fixed to the High Girders themselves.

During construction the third contractors established a foundry at Wormit Bay. Left almost entirely under the control of a single foreman, Fergus Ferguson, the metal bought in was of mediocre quality, while the moulds and cores were improperly prepared. As a result the castings produced were of variable quality with many columns having uneven wall thickness. Early-on these were identified, scrapped and replaced, 30-40 and more at a time. But as more and more metalwork had flaws this quality control became unrealistic and, unbeknownst to the senior managers, only the very worst were scrapped. As for the pier columns, it was difficult to cast the main sections with the brace securing

The last standing northern pier, demonstrating the bridge's height up to the underside of the (fallen) High Girders. *The National Library of Scotland, Shelfmark Phot.la.17, Creative Commons Attribution 4.0 International Licence*

THE BRIDGE IS DOWN!'

The Tay Bridge from the south. *The National Library of Scotland, Shelfmark Phot.la.17, Creative Commons Attribution 4.0 International Licence*

lugs in one piece. Where these had miscast, separate lugs were 'burned' on in a forerunner to welding. Management knew of this, but later claimed they thought this was part of construction lifting supports and not the actual bridge structure. Gilkes' contract with the NBR detailed that work was to be approved by Bouch; there is no satisfactory evidence that he or his representatives ever properly did so.

One final noteworthy issue occurred during construction. In February 1877 two of the High Girders, Nos. 12 and 13, were being lifted into place when a storm erupted. Before they could be secured they broke free and fell into the river. Rather than being replaced, these large and costly structures were repaired and hauled back into position.

As the 'rainbow bridge' was pushing the boundaries of civil engineering, it and Bouch became world famous, with General Grant specifically detouring his UK tour to visit it under construction. He later described it simply as 'a very long bridge'.

When completed the bridge was 2 miles long, 169 feet high, had 85 piers, carried a single track and cost £300,000. It was the longest in the world, and one of the tallest, requiring:

The semi-collapsed Pier No. 3 looking east, demonstrating column braces and attachment lugs. *The National Library of Scotland, Shelfmark Phot.la.17, Creative Commons Attribution 4.0 International Licence*

3700 tons of cast iron
3500 tons of malleable iron
87,000 cubic feet of timber
15,000 casks of cement
Ten million bricks
Two million rivets
And cost 20 lives

Signal boxes were constructed at each end and Dundee gained the so-named 'Tay Bridge Station' connecting with the Caledonian Railway. Major-General Hutchinson of the Board of Trade undertook tests, running engines up to 40mph across. He recommended a maximum speed limit of 25mph and declared the bridge safe. He aimed to return to see the effects of the wind on a train, but never did.

The bridge was opened on 31st May 1878 to great public acclaim, although Queen Victoria did not attend. She did, however, cross on 20th June 1879 after insisting that her royal train be taken empty over it several times to ensure it was safe…

The completion of the Tay Bridge made the names of those associated with it. Head foreman Albert Grothe had a successful lecture tour explaining the construction, while after Victoria's crossing Bouch was knighted for his work. Showered with praise, he was also given the contract to construct his intended bridge across the Forth. As McGonagall's first poem recalled:

'Beautiful Railway Bridge of the Silvery Tay!
And prosperity to Messrs Bouche and Grothe,

The Tay Bridge viewed from the north (note the central High Girders). *The National Library of Scotland, Shelfmark Phot.la.17, Creative Commons Attribution 4.0 International Licence*

The famous engineers of the present day,
Who have succeeded in erecting the Railway
Bridge of the Silvery Tay,
Which stands unequalled to be seen
Near by Dundee and the Magdalen Green.'

The NBR's gamble had paid off – traffic boomed with the bridge and while the single track was slow and the ninepence crossing fare generated complaints, the company soon overtook the Caledonian as Scotland's premier railway. But there were difficulties. Many heard strange noises, almost like electric crackles, emanating from the bridge. Passengers noticed high speeds – one calculating approximately 42mph – while the bridge began swaying both vertically and laterally by up to two inches. Purportedly this worsened when entering the High Girders, especially those that fell during construction. Occasionally columns making up the piers cracked due to expanding cement and had to be bound with hoops. Most worrying, not that anyone at the time paid attention, were the undersized bolts that let parts slide over each other as they worked loose, many bolts falling free altogether. As one worker said of the column braces, it was *'about as slovenly a piece of work as ever I saw in my life'*.

The bridge was not maintained by the NBR; instead Bouch was to supervise this. He hired Henry Noble, who had helped construction, as Bridge Inspector despite being a bricklayer with no experience of metal structures. Concentrating on the piers and brickwork, he also inspected the ironwork – not technically his job but nobody else had been hired to do this. When checking the piers for scour he noted various braces were 'chattering' as they had worked loose and were no longer under tension – another design issue. Believing the metal wedges used, known as 'cotters', were too small he bought a rod of metal and, cutting it into packing shims, pushed these into the gaps where he could not tighten them up any more. He never told Bouch of the issue. The trains kept running and the 'rainbow bridge' was an irrefutable monument to 'limitless' Victorian engineering.

The year passed, and with New Year beckoning travellers began returning

The semi-collapsed Pier No. 1 looking south, showing how little of the bridge structure actually comprised brickwork. *The National Library of Scotland, Shelfmark Phot.la.17, Creative Commons Attribution 4.0 International Licence*

homewards. On 28th December 1879 the 1:30pm mail train from Dundee to Burntisland was set to depart, but the tank engine that should have taken it (No. 89 *Ladybank* of the '88' Class) failed, so Driver David Mitchell and Fireman John Marshall took Wheatley-designed No. 224 as a replacement. Built in 1871 for express passenger trains it was Britain's first inside-cylinder 4-4-0, but as trains were getting heavier the Class was becoming outmoded. Comprising three Third Class coaches, one First Class, one Second Class and a Brakevan, the journey and Tay crossing was completed without incident and at 5:20pm the return trip from Burntisland to Dundee commenced, aiming to arrive around 7:30pm. That evening a storm began to brew, building up in strength. Hitting Dundee around 5:30pm, roofs across the area were damaged, chimneys smashed, trees uprooted and in the sidings at Wormit Bay full coal wagons started to roll up the gradient, pushed by the wind.

Stopping at Saint Fort Station, tickets were checked. Most passengers were travelling alone but there were exceptions: the Watson family (father and two sons), Schoolmaster Neish with his daughter, and two sweethearts – Eliza Smart and George Johnston. Boarding at Saint Fort, he was only on the train to spend some time with her. As the train approached the southern signalbox at Wormit Bay it slowed so Mitchell could pick up the token permitting them to cross the bridge. The storm was at its height: winds over 70mph; thick black clouds blocking out the moon; driving rain cutting across the open-cabbed engine. They moved forwards onto the bridge. Around 7:13pm several people on the banks saw the faint lights of the train and brief flashes of sparks. Then nothing.

James Smith, Tay Bridge Station Master, was waiting for No. 224. The train was late, and the telegraph across the bridge between the signalboxes had gone dead. Already people were shouting 'the bridge is down' and 'there's a train into the water'. Dundee locomotive foreman James Roberts ran up, saying he'd heard similar. Deciding to cross the bridge for themselves, Smith stopped partway, giddy and blinded, but Roberts continued. The storm forced him to his knees, so he crawled through the rain. Feeling ahead of him, he followed the rails until he reached out at thin air. The moon momentarily lit up the area and Roberts looked out over the Tay. The High Girders were gone.

News spread rapidly and a crowd formed at Tay Bridge Station. Many at home with telescopes trained in on the bridge, only it was no longer there.

Cabinet card showing the fallen High Girders and the severed southern half of the bridge in the background. *Author's collection*

James Roberts at the northernmost edge of the broken bridge. © Illustrated London News/*Mary Evans Picture Library*

The Harbour Master and railway officials took the ferry out to see for themselves, hoping they could hear survivors over the storm. The lifeboat was called, but to no avail. Bouch was telegraphed and set off immediately.

With rumour abounding as to the number of victims, the official figures were only ascertained when Robert Mores, Station Agent at Saint Fort arrived by ferry.

View from the south of the broken piers (mirroring the *Illustrated London News* engraving).
The National Library of Scotland, Shelfmark Phot.la.17, Creative Commons Attribution 4.0 International Licence

With him he brought 57 ticket stubs, recalling an additional two season tickets and around 11 retained tickets. At the time it was thought 75 were aboard, but recent research suggests the train may have actually contained 59. No survivors were found.

With the Monday morning the disaster was headline news nation-wide – the first real shock to Victorian confidence in engineering. Formerly a source of national pride, this was – and remains – the only case of a British railway accident without a single survivor. As details emerged, the ensuing anger and confusion was immense. For a comparison, this really was the Victorian's *Titanic*.

A fleet of boats left Dundee early on Monday to the scene, one carrying Harbour Diver Edward Simpson. The water visibility was poor and the only section he found did not contain the train. Board of Trade representatives were despatched; the Queen telegraphed her sympathies. Bouch arrived shortly with his son, being informed of what little was known. Already many were openly blaming him. At 10am he and NBR officials reached the bridge, while more divers were called for. All NBR through services via Aberdeen were suspended and the Tay Bridge Station refreshment room was prepared as a mortuary. Station Master Smith kept the crowds informed, and that evening the body of Ann Cruikshank was found 3 miles downriver – the first victim recovered. Later offering five pounds per body recovered (subsequently reduced to two pounds), 46 were eventually found in the following weeks, including David Johnston (one of the Guards), Fireman John Marshall and Driver David Mitchell, who left a wife and five young children.

Divers found the carriages on Tuesday; the locomotive on Wednesday. Lying in a relatively straight line to the east of the piers, the High Girders were near entirely underwater with the smashed train still inside. Unlike in illustrations, the train did not fly off a precipice, actually being trapped inside this falling cage. As body recovery turned to salvage some girders were lifted, but it was slow and some required dynamiting, destroying any evidence they may have held. The Council formed a relief fund to aid relatives. Collecting over £3300, this included £500 from the NBR, another £500 independently from its Directors and £250 from Bouch. Although NBR shares had dropped already Chairman John Stirling declared 'the Tay will again be bridged'. The Forth Bridge plans were swiftly halted and Bouch removed from the project.

On 3rd January 1880 the Inquiry commenced in Dundee. It was chaired by Henry Rothery, Commissioner of Wrecks; Colonel William Yolland, Inspector of Railways and William Barlow, President of the Institute of Civil Engineers. Engineer Henry Law was appointed to undertake detailed investigation, while James Brunlees and John Cochrane were similarly appointed by the NBR. On conclusion of their

A salvaged High Girder section containing part of the wrecked train. *The National Library of Scotland, Shelfmark Phot.la.17, Creative Commons Attribution 4.0 International Licence*

report, claiming deficiencies in design and workmanship, the Inquiry resumed in Westminster, concluding on 8th May. As there was no set focus such as identifying the exact cause or allocating blame, there was disagreement and much was overlooked. Ultimately there were two separate reports – one by Yolland and Barlow, citing numerous responsibilities, and another by Rothery – placing blame squarely on Bouch.

While small debris and a few girders were brought up almost immediately, it was only by April 1880 that the engine and carriages were raised, while the remaining girders were salvaged over the following years. The NBR financed a replacement bridge, constructed by the Arrol Company to a design by Barlow, but the NBR never fully recovered. Opened on 13th July 1887, the new bridge had deeper foundations, broader supports carrying two tracks, greater overall strength and it remains in use today, although trains are suspended in exceptional winds. As McGonagall described in his last Tay poem:

'Beautiful New Railway Bridge of the Silvery Tay,
With your strong brick piers and buttresses in so grand array,
And your thirteen central girders, which seem to my eye
Strong enough all windy storms to defy.'

The Arrol Firm also completed the Forth Rail Bridge in 1890, *not* to Bouch's design. Instead, it was designed by Sir John Fowler and Sir Benjamin Baker.

Another bridge Bouch and Gilkes the contractors were completing at the time of the disaster – the South Esk Viaduct – was inspected, declared even more dangerous than the Tay Bridge, condemned and demolished before it ever carried a commercial train. Similarly his Redheugh Bridge in Newcastle was condemned in 1896. Bouch died a broken man, his reputation destroyed, on 30th October 1880 – barely four months after the final reports. The surviving end girders of the ruined bridge were reused on the new bridge and the supporting columns demolished. As geologists accidentally discovered in 1994, some portions are still on the bottom. The piers themselves remain visible even at high tide and are considered by many to be 'tombstones' for those never recovered.

The disaster greatly affected Dundee, and although a memorial at the site was only unveiled in 2013 the events of that storm remain in folklore, most distinctly with stories of ghostly carriage lights slowly passing along the bridge every anniversary, only to disappear in the centre...

The new Tay Bridge alongside the piers of its ill-fated predecessor. *Chris McKenna, Creative Commons Attribution-Share Alike 4.0 International license*

So what was the cause of the disaster? The Inquiry covered many angles in great detail, ultimately identifying several central factors amid many smaller issues.

As already noted, plans had to be changed when the survey was found to be wrong, and changing contractors worsened the issue. While the piers themselves were stable, they were too narrow; the cement had poor adhesion while the columns' foundations were too small for their height and broke through. In fact the columns and High Girders – the latter perfectly acceptable in themselves – had bodily moved 20 inches before falling.

Wind pressure with hindsight was particularly important. Not fully recognised at the time, it was not required by the Board of Trade to check lattice bridge girders so no specific calculations were made. Grothe believed that the bridge was capable of withstanding a gale akin to the 1859 'Royal Charter Storm', around 21 pounds per square foot, thought to be the worst the British weather could ever get. The first time this particular storm was surpassed – potentially by over double – was the last Sabbath day of 1879. Later Bouch declared that he considered the wind resistance calculations for his proposed Forth Bridge to have been appropriate: ten pounds per square foot. Other engineers at the Inquiry argued that – construction issues aside – it *should* have been designed to cope with at least 20 pounds per square foot, if not 30 or even 50, and that if these parameters were exceeded the bridge ought to have toppled rather than physically collapsing. Construction though reduced any design capabilities – Cochrane even stating were it not for this it 'would be standing now'. Poorly constructed with loose components, the bridge underwent uneven loading so increasing internal stresses. A Wind Pressure Commission was established as a result to consider wind loading for future bridge designs.

As for the columns themselves, they encapsulated the fundamental dangers resulting from the insufficiently supervised Wormit foundry. While testing proved the bolts and iron itself to be acceptable – not good, but passable – parts were very poorly cast. The columns had uneven wall thickness, creating irregular stresses which even Bouch criticised at the Inquiry. The bolts holding the sections together were too small, allowing the parts to slide over each other. The number of braces was also wholly insufficient and they became slack through flawed design, further working loose due to their attaching lugs.

These lugs were central to the collapse mechanism – all detached braces failed by the lugs giving way. Burned on separately where miscast, they were massively unsound and terribly weak even when successfully cast. Additionally, the holes in the lugs were cast rather than drilled, so were not uniform and in fact had a

Diagram showing how bracing attachment lugs failed. *Author*

conical taper – increasing stresses when under tension, causing bolts to bend and slacken. Again, Bouch retrospectively criticised this. These all reduced the loads they could withstand and when tested it was found they failed when loaded to about 20 tons, well below what was expected. On top of this, for over a year they had been placed under more and more strain as the bridge vibrated

Pier No. 7 looking west, showing examples of broken lugs on all three column bases visible. *The National Library of Scotland, Shelfmark Phot.la.17, Creative Commons Attribution 4.0 International Licence*

and the bolts were padded with metal shims. When these components failed, the pier columns essentially disassembled, tipping the unattached girders over into the Tay.

The bridge's components were obviously fatally poor. But it gets worse. In addition, there were huge numbers of manufacturing flaws – blow holes, cracks and gaps. One worker even described some pieces as looking 'honeycombed'. Those that were obviously no good were recast, but so many parts had faults that Foreman Ferguson, in near-sole charge, adopted an alternate policy unknown to Grothe. To save time and money, any issue that looked unsightly was filled with a material called 'Beaumont's Egg'. Essentially a filler, this compound consisted of iron filings, beeswax, resin and lamp black (fine soot) mixed together and painted when hardened – and a *lot* was used. The treated metalwork was plainly not as strong as properly-cast parts, so 'Beaumont's Egg', masking blemishes and dangerous weaknesses, was also in essence acting as a stabilising agent. As the bridge vibrated though, stress was placed on the egg filler which cracked and fell apart, so transferring further stress to the flaws.

'Beaumont's Egg' was quite literally glossing over the cracks: faulty castings were disguised using a material with the structural integrity of glass. More importantly, *they knew*. This was not a question of unknown weaknesses or hidden issues – workers found these flaws and actively hid them, not just by using filler but by then hiding components under tarpaulins so Grothe would not see them. They *knew* the bridge was compromised.

A period home-made souvenir made from Tay Bridge carriage debris.
Author's collection

This slovenly workmanship and poor design, particularly concerning wind resistance, was exacerbated by high train speeds (which drivers denied), the fall of two girders during construction, the provision of a maintenance man with no experience of iron structures and his adding of packing pieces to rattling joints rather than seeking advice. Collectively these all let the bridge ever-increasingly vibrate and sway until the stresses became too great. Clichéd as it may be, the bridge was doomed to fall.

Bouch's design may have been flawed but his errors were compounded by advisors who took shortcuts, inaccurate surveyors, poor contractors, worse foundrymen and excessive train speeds. With so many individual factors, Rothery ultimately stated:

> 'The conclusion then, to which we have come, is that this bridge was badly designed, badly constructed, and badly maintained, and that its downfall was due to inherent defects in the structure, which must sooner or later have brought it down. For these defects both in the design, the construction, and the maintenance, Sir Thomas Bouch is, in our opinion, mainly to blame.'

So we have an iron bridge with a perpetually-modified design, maintained by a bricklayer and held together with wax. The reasons for the collapse are plain – clearly with hindsight it could have fallen down at any moment, which raises an incredibly important question. Why did it fall down *then*?

Now all disasters are the result of a chain of factors, but all require a final catalyst. Without it all other factors in the chain would have no combined effect, and that includes compromised design.

The catalyst for the Tay Bridge Disaster has been the centre of debate ever since. Most simple is Rothery's conclusion that the wind was just too great with the cumulative stress. Yolland and Barlow remained somewhat vague, allowing that a column may have fractured through shockwave. Others have said that the use of the larger No. 224 rather than the regular engine increased wind resistance past design limits. Some say the bridge could have been hit by a water spout, while others at the time claimed it was God's punishment for travelling on the Sabbath. Whatever it was, it was rapid – the engine's regulator was still wide open and the brakes off.

The current popular claim, originally proffered by Bouch, was that the Second Class coach just before the last van derailed and the shockwave from this that caused the lugs to fail. This claim directly led to debate on the overall significance of wind resistance on the disaster. The period view was that the carriage was literally blown over by the wind. Others have since suggested that it derailed where the dropped girder caused a 'nod' in the track, only striking the bridge itself further in at a support.

But there is no solid evidence for any of this. Eye witness accounts described sparks coming from the front of the train, not the carriage wheels as the previous train's guard had described. All the carriages were badly smashed, but uniformly and without any clear evidence of collision. Any girder damage has to be discounted in no small part through dynamiting. Various impact marks were put forward by Bouch,

One of the destroyed coaches after salvage.
The National Library of Scotland, Shelfmark Phot.la.17,
Creative Commons Attribution 4.0 International Licence

but these were at best circumstantial. Arguably most telling, not one person called at the Inquiry had ever seen or heard of a railway carriage being blown over. Forth Bridge designer Benjamin Baker did not dismiss a derailment, but particularly with anti-derailment guard rails on the bridge suggested *if* it occurred it was probably for entirely different reasons than the wind.

Whether through impact shockwave or cumulative overloading, all that is known for certain is that when the train was a third of the way through the High Girders many of the lugs holding the pier columns together failed en-masse, pitching the High Girders over.

However, there *is* evidence for the cause of the disaster – a cause no one has previously considered. Everyone aboard the train was lost but, as the locals still say, there was one survivor, and her account has been all but ignored.

Falling with the High Girders to the riverbed, locomotive No. 224 was found by divers three days later. Originally described as in good condition, a salvage barge trailing its anchor struck her, destroying the cab, damaging the boiler

Locomotive 224 after salvage. *The National Library of Scotland, Shelfmark Phot.la.17, Creative Commons Attribution 4.0 International Licence*

cladding and dome, and probably destroying the funnel. Later chains were attached to her for salvage, but they parted and she sank again. Finally recovered after a second attempt, she was photographed for the Inquiry then taken to Cowlairs in Glasgow to be repaired, being given the nickname of 'The Diver'. She subsequently ran for over forty years, though it was only in 1908 that a driver dared to take her over the new Tay Bridge. In 1919 she was withdrawn and scrapped.

The photographs taken of No. 224's damage have been frequently reproduced, but all who have seen them have made an assumption – a logical one, but wrong. For without that assumption the story of the Tay Bridge Disaster takes a very different direction. And that assumption is that No. 224 was damaged *during the collapse* of the Tay Bridge.

Clearly to some degree the assumption is of course correct, but consider for a moment that that was unknown. Modern forensic disaster investigations adopt a principle where all pieces of evidence are recovered and examined, aiming to reverse engineer how it broke apart – something unheard of in 1879. Several have undertaken analysis of this form, but always looking at the bridge, never the locomotive. So using this modern principle, what can these photographs reveal of the causes of the damage inflicted to No. 224?

First to consider is the right-hand side that was lying downwards in contact with the bridge on the riverbed. Discounting salvage damage, comparison of buckled areas with the girders clearly shows a correlation where the engine struck mid-fall, while scrapes along the engine show its forward movement while in contact with the girders during the fall. As for the crushed cab side, it

Right-hand side of No. 224 showing salvage damage (red) and collapse damage (yellow). *Author, based on the original from The National Library of Scotland, Shelfmark Phot.la.17, Creative Commons Attribution 4.0 International Licence*

perfectly matches the curved shape of the tender handbrake lever – the coupling between engine and tender having broken. Obviously, impacts across a large area resulted in multiple damage points – none were independent – and all the right-hand side damage was caused either by the fall or the salvage.

With an engine moving forwards on a bridge that collapsed to the right, with the engine landing on its right-hand side, it would be logical for the majority of the damage to be on the engine's right, more specifically with the peak of damage being to the front right corner (the buffer beam) as it moved forwards. But as the photographs reveal, the left-hand side has substantially more damage – the running board bent upwards and torn free from the main frames while the left buffer, rail guard and an entire portion of the buffer beam were snapped off entirely. The hypothesis of the worst damage being to the right is completely wrong. So what caused this?

Using other accidents as contextual precedents, the answer is clear – it is the impact damage that should have been on the right as suggested and – more impor-tantly – it is near-identical to that expected from a collision. As said, the greatest damage is always at the first point of impact, so small surprise there was no clear evidence on the carriages – it was the *engine* that derailed.

Left-hand side of No. 224 showing salvage damage (red), collapse damage (yellow) and pre-collapse damage (blue). *Author, based on the original from The National Library of Scotland, Shelfmark Phot.la.17, Creative Commons Attribution 4.0 International Licence*

With all but the last driving wheels off the track, No. 224 would have dropped downwards and leant sideways, easily reaching across to the girders. At this new angle the bend to the running board matches the upward slant of the girders. Furthermore, striking an inclined girder as the train

The derailed No. 224 in relation to the bridge girders. *Author, based on the original from The National Library of Scotland, Shelfmark Phot.la.17, Creative Commons Attribution 4.0 International Licence*

moved forwards would have acted as a wedge, separating running board and frames as photographed. This would have also easily snapped off the buffer in a twisting motion, explaining horizontal cracks to the surviving portion. As for the twisted upper running board section, this would have hit the girder on the left in a similar manner to that on the right during the fall itself.

What must be remembered – this all occurred *before* the bridge collapsed. How do we know? The bridge fell to the right – which coincidentally explains the damage to the surviving rail guard, striking the rail as the engine slid from left to right in the instant of the collapse. There were no bridge remains to the

Front view of No. 224 with highlighted damage
(note the twisted and snapped bufferbeam).
Author, based on the original from The National Library of
Scotland, Shelfmark Phot.la.17, Creative Commons
Attribution 4.0 International Licence

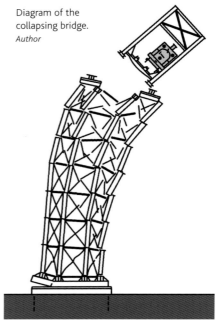

Diagram of the
collapsing bridge.
Author

west of the piers – it did not disintegrate in that direction, so left-hand side
damage had to precede falling to the right. The only alternative would be falling
debris, but the necessary debris would have to have struck sideways not
downwards – thus contrary to gravity – and there would have been other
damaged areas (such as to the smokebox or frames), which is not present. A
frontal collision would also explain the brief flurry of sparks witnessed coming
from the front of the train, and as the footplate suddenly pitched over the crew
would have lost balance, hence not closing the regulator or applying the brakes.
This is grimly demonstrated by burns on the face of Fireman Marshall. Furthermore, the records state that while the High Girders fell intact, the area on No.
224's left was 'very much broken'.

So the bridge collapsed because of internal weaknesses worsened by a storm,
stressed further by a large train that suddenly derailed and struck the girders,
sending shockwaves to the lugs. There is clear photographic evidence for this
collision between engine and girders that no-one has previously identified. But
is this the catalyst? No, because it raises one final question. Why did the engine
derail? At over 56 tons it certainly was not the wind, and the derailment
occurred in the opposite direction to the wind in any event.

This is where conjecture takes over: the engine has been long since scrapped
and the only surviving evidence are the photographs, but they give a strong clue
to another part of the theory.

As locomotive designs developed, engines and boilers got bigger and longer. Rigid wheelbases can only be so long and still go round curves, so separate unpowered supporting wheels capable of pivoting were introduced. Those with four or more wheels are referred to as 'bogies'. As a 4-4-0, No. 224 had a leading bogie with four wheels, four driving wheels and no trailing support wheels. This wheel layout limited size so was later discontinued, along with having cases of rocking oscillation. This rocking issue was the very reason Wheatley developed No. 224 with inside cylinders in an attempt to combat it.

Describing the photographed right hand bogie side first, each axle was supported on either end of a large leaf spring for suspension. To keep tension on it a stretcher ran from axlebox to axlebox, its rear portion extending beyond the axle (likely a counterweight, collectively ensuring the wheels remained in contact with the rails).

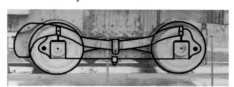

Extract showing the right hand bogie side of No. 224 (some components outlined for clarity). *Author, based on the original from The National Library of Scotland, Shelfmark Phot.la.17, Creative Commons Attribution 4.0 International Licence*

But in photographs the left-hand bogie side fails to match. The stretcher is cleanly broken, drooping downwards to rail level, while the rearmost portion is missing altogether. The wheels, frames and spring show no sign of impact or any damage whatsoever, so this was not the result of falling debris. Salvage chains went around the boiler not the bogie, so it was not due to that. As the collision damage was confined to the running board it cannot have originated there either.

Extract showing the left hand bogie side of No. 224 with broken components (blue). *Author, based on the original from The National Library of Scotland, Shelfmark Phot.la.17, Creative Commons Attribution 4.0 International Licence*

So what could have caused it? One hypothesis stands out. As the engine travelled the axleboxes and springs moved vertically, as was their intention, with the stretcher offering resistance to keep the wheels on the track. But some flex would have been transferred to this component, particularly with engine oscillation, while bumpy track – notably when daily crossing the Tay Bridge – would have made this flexing greater. Unknown at the time, this is the prime cause of metal fatigue. Whether the stretcher was faulty or not is unknown and unwise to speculate, but after circa nine years of operation an unexpected component failure is not impossible, and the photographs undeniably show it broke very cleanly without any obvious explanation.

To rewind to 7:13pm, 28th December 1879, this is how the 'rainbow bridge' most probably met its end.

NBR No. 224, hauling six coaches entered the High Girders. The bridge was swaying as badly as usual, if not worse, and this was greatest in this area. The increasing stress on the bogie stretcher – weakened after years of flexing – was too great and the rear portion cracked and fell off. With the right half of the bogie axles under pressure while the left half suddenly lost this weight, the left side jarred upwards. This final twist was just sufficient to crack the centre of the stretcher, and the rear portion dropped down to rail height.

But the rails on the bridge were different: there were two for running and two inner guard rails to prevent derailments. The position of this broken stretcher, as in the photograph, would have made it drop between these rails, so with the forward momentum of the train it would have struck head-on one of the 'chairs' holding the rails in place. With an unstoppable force meeting an immovable object, the stretcher would have acted like a lever, lifting the bogie and engine upwards. If lifted to only two degrees all bar the rear driving wheels would have been clear of the track. Pitching at an angle, the crew were knocked over and the stretcher disengaged as the engine dropped to the floor, some three degrees down. It struck the girders on the left, tearing the running board as it ran up the inclining beam. Not a major collision, most of the damage was cosmetic.

The bridge though not only had a shockwave run through it, but the collision would have momentarily put uneven pressure on the columns. Those to the left would have been compressed as the bridge rocked towards the wind, while

Inside the High Girders (note the track composing running and guard rails). *The National Library of Scotland, Shelfmark Phot.la.17, Creative Commons Attribution 4.0 International Licence*

those to the right would have been put under sudden tension, snapping the lugs. As the bridge recoiled, aided by the wind, the train slid to the right, causing the tension and compression to be reversed. Broken lugs released braces on the right, followed almost instantly by lugs failing on the left. Crumpling and already collapsing, the High Girders were thrown out to the right, supported by no more than the wind. With the engine sliding slightly forwards in the falling girders, the final left-hand damage was caused by falling debris, and darkness fell over the Tay.

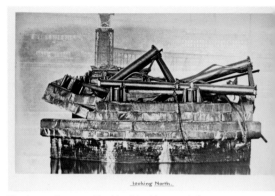

The force of nature: Pier No. 5 looking north (note the brickwork torn upwards during the collapse). *The National Library of Scotland, Shelfmark Phot.la.17, Creative Commons Attribution 4.0 International Licence*

This is a completely new theory and open for debate, but two things are certain. No. 224 collided with the bridge on the left, and the broken bogie spacer fouled the track. Unlike other theories, this has clear and unequivocal photographic evidence. Finally, could striking an upper girder really demolish a bridge? Yes – because it still happens. As but one example, on 24th May 2013 an American road bridge over the Skagit river collapsed after being struck by a lorry.

The Tay Bridge Disaster is a warning against overconfidence and cutting corners. But from a historical perspective it also forewarns against making assumptions – hindsight can be a dangerous thing.

Bouch was rightly to blame, but the fault was not his alone. The contractors compromised his bridge quite apart from the problems of his design, and collectively these issues destined the final outcome. But this new theory changes our perspective slightly. True, engineering had been pushed too far and Victorian faith was misplaced, but the timing was a complete fluke. The irony is that the final factor that led to this greatest of railway disasters was the failure of a component in a locomotive that had been well designed and properly built, but was just in the wrong place at the wrong time. Any other bridge would have coped, as might the Tay Bridge. To quote McGonagall:

'Had they been supported on each side with buttresses,
At least many sensible men confesses,
For the stronger we our houses do build,
The less chance we have of being killed.'

'HOY, HOY, WHERE ARE YOU COMING TO?'
The *Princess Alice* Disaster

The *Princess Alice*. © Illustrated London News/*Mary Evans Picture Library*

The tragic collision on the River Thames between the vessels *Marchioness* and *Bowbelle* in 1989 is well within living memory and still regularly referred to in Parliament and the Press. Yet the equally terrible collision between the steamer *Princess Alice* and the collier *Bywell Castle* appears virtually unknown, in spite of holding a grim record – the worst disaster on the Thames. Nonetheless, the description of a crowded passenger vessel struck down mid-voyage by a significantly larger merchant ship within sight of London, resulting in great loss of life, is sadly echoed by both disasters.

The paddle steamer *Princess Alice* was built in 1865 by Messrs Caird of Greenock, originally named *Bute*. She operated on the Clyde for the Wemyss Bay Steamboat Company until 1867 when purchased by the Woolwich Steamboat Company, who strengthened and refitted her with a large saloon deck for Thames excursions carrying day-trippers to Sheerness. In 1873 she was used to take the Shah of Persia from the Tower of London to West India Docks, a duty that gave her much local publicity and the nickname of 'The Shah's Boat'. However, that October while anchored off Woolwich in fog a waterman's boat was forced under her stern by the tide and capsized, killing nine people. It was the memory of this accident which led to the Woolwich Tunnel, opened in 1912. In 1876 all the small Thames steamboat companies were amalgamated into one: the London Steamboat Company under the ownership of John Orwell Lever. This included *Princess Alice* and her sister ship *Duke of Teck*. In early 1878 she was overhauled and fitted with new boilers.

With an overall tonnage of 251 gross tons, *Princess Alice* was 254 feet long, 35 feet wide over her paddle boxes and permitted to carry 936 passengers. A comparatively ordinary design, the most important facet to consider was her navigational layout. She was steered from a wheel located above the saloons between the two funnels, the centre of the vessel, with the main Bridge directly overhead stretching across the ship. Visibility from the wheel was virtually zero, being blocked by the forward funnel and worsened by the length of the vessel, with the helmsman relying entirely upon orders from the captain on the Bridge. But visibility from the bridge was also hampered for the same basic reasons, so the captain had to rely on lookouts at the bow. The result was a potentially significant time lag between the lookout sighting an obstacle, informing the Bridge, the commander deciding a course of action, ordering the helmsman and only then the helmsman actually turning.

In 1876 *Princess Alice* gained a new captain: Robert William Grinstead. He had risen through the ranks, starting out as an apprentice and working up to be a fully qualified Thames waterman, being highly respected:

'…his unremitting care and knowledge of how to handle a long, unhandy vessel were beyond all praise.'

George Long was the first mate while Henry Young and John Rand were lookouts. Both lookouts were inexperienced; Young had only worked on board for three days and was unaccustomed to the ship and route. Arguably the most important figure concerning the forthcoming disaster was John Eyres. Information on him varies – even his account at the Inquiry changed regularly. He was officially a passenger, and friends with the regular helmsman, Hopgood. When Hopgood requested to disembark at Gravesend, Grinstead permitted Eyres to take over as helmsman. It was later found that Eyres, whilst an experienced seaman, had never before steered a ship the size of *Princess Alice* nor had ever steered a vessel on the Thames. Many vessels around this time had to use specialist pilots familiar with the river when navigating, however, *Princess Alice* was exempt from this requirement. This exemption was for the ship itself though – *not* any member of the crew operating her…

The other vessel involved in the calamity was the *Bywell Castle*, an ocean-going collier built in 1870 by Messrs Palmer of Jarrow. Little information exists on her career prior to the disaster, but her owners, the Hall Brothers, operated primarily between Newcastle and the Mediterranean carrying coal and cargo. At 256 feet long and 32 feet in beam (width), she may not appear to have been that much larger than *Princess Alice*, yet she was equipped for steam and sail propulsion and was remarked as being quite a tall ship, especially when unloaded, towering over small river steamers. Furthermore, weighing 1376 gross tons, *Bywell Castle* was five times heavier than *Princess Alice*. As with

The *Bywell Castle* after the collision. © Illustrated London News/*Mary Evans Picture Library*

Princess Alice, her Bridge was central with the wheel beneath, but her single funnel was behind this position.

Her captain was Thomas Harrison. An experienced Master, having been at sea for thirty-seven years, he was also a part-owner of the ship. His ship was exempt from needing a pilot, but he was unfamiliar with the Thames so the Company hired Christopher Dix. A pilot for thirty-four years, Dix was fully qualified, although Harrison disliked him. While the captain of a vessel under pilot usually left the Bridge, command of the vessel transferring over, Harrison kept a close eye on Dix's orders and remained by his side. The remainder of the crew was made up of 'runners' – seamen who ran individual coastal trips and were not contracted to any particular ship.

On 3rd September 1878, *Princess Alice* sailed on her regular excursion trip from Tower Bridge to Sheerness via Blackwell, North Woolwich, Rosherville Gardens and Gravesend. With an almost full complement of passengers – mostly working class – the voyage was uneventful, passengers and crew spending a pleasant day at Sheerness before beginning the return journey at 4:15pm. With the sun setting, at 6:30pm she left Rosherville Pier having picked up more passengers before heading upriver for Woolwich, working against the ebbing tide. Grinstead was standing on the Bridge, Eyres at the helm, lookouts Long and Young near the forward funnel and lookout Rand at the bow. On board were approximately 800 passengers; there was no passenger list, so the exact number is unknown. With music and dancing, it is likely the crew were somewhat distracted. As was typical, there was no emergency drill of any description.

Early in the return trip *Princess Alice* was almost involved in a collision with a brigantine sailing vessel, but reversed her engines in time. Such encounters were common; river navigational rules were almost non-existent with vessels usually darting from one bank to another to catch the tide. Some obeyed the 'Rule of the Road' – the policy of passing port-to-port (left-hand side to left-hand side) – but it was not compulsory, only being law for designated ocean shipping lanes. At North Fleet Hope she was forced to stop for five minutes due to the boilers priming (water bubbling over into the cylinders), and at this time her navigational lights were lit. By 7:45pm she neared Tripcock Point, Woolwich, and starboarded her helm upon passing another steamer.

Meanwhile, *Bywell Castle* was moored up at Millwall Dock on the Isle of Dogs. Not a regular Thames vessel, she was only in London for a repaint, and due to congestion around the docks she was unable to depart until the evening ebb tide.

During the wait Dix arranged a temporary crew of 'runners'. At 6:30pm she slowly reversed out of the dry dock, but a barge broke its moorings and drifted into her path. Being unloaded, her rotating propeller was partially out of the water and struck the barge, causing minor damage to the latter. After leaving the dock her navigational lights were lit and she sailed down river at half-speed,

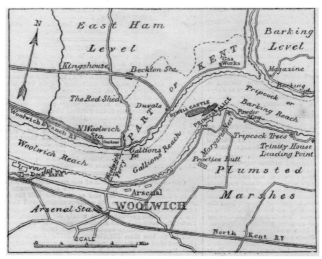

Map showing the location of the collision. © Illustrated London News/*Mary Evans Picture Library*

sailing with the tide, heading for Newcastle. Harrison and Dix were on the bridge and a 'runner' called Hardy was acting as lookout at the bow. Around 7:45pm she neared Tripcock Point, keeping watch for other shipping – mostly moored ships on the south bank and the Woolwich floating powder magazine.

According to the Board of Trade Inquiry, at approximately 7:45pm *Bywell Castle* and *Princess Alice* spotted each other – captains and lookouts sighting each vessel simultaneously. On *Bywell Castle*, Harrison was asked whether he saw 'the red light', probably by lookout Hardy, while on *Princess Alice* lookout Long did not report the vessel. As *Princess Alice* neared Tripcock Point she starboarded her helm and momentarily slowed. Sailing in the opposite direction, *Bywell Castle* maintained her speed and planned course, porting her helm very slightly with the intention of passing port–to–port, keeping *Princess Alice's* red light in view. *Bywell Castle* then straightened her helm, believing that *Princess Alice* would do likewise.

What happened next has never been fully ascertained, but it appears that Eyres – inexperienced at handling such a vessel – failed to straighten *Princess Alice's* course and lost control in the ebbing tide. She swung to port, being pushed across the course of *Bywell Castle* – Long suddenly realising that he was looking directly end-on to the oncoming collier. At that moment Grinstead ordered the engines stopped before shouting across to *Bywell Castle*:

'*Hoy, Hoy, Where are you coming to?*'

Harrison, however, realised the danger and had already taken over from Dix – ordering the engines reversed and the helm starboarded in the hope that the vessels might pass starboard–to–starboard. But it was not to be.

Amid shouts and screams as the giant vessel loomed overhead, at 7:55pm the knife-like bow of *Bywell Castle* struck *Princess Alice* just in front of the starboard paddle box. Slicing 17 feet into her hull, almost two thirds of the steamer's overall width, the first real resistance *Princess Alice* gave was when the main steam pipe was struck. While some passengers described it as a 'comfortable blow', this belied its true damage; as Harrison put it:

'The other vessel was just like an eggshell.'

The sudden ingress of water into her engine room, coupled with the strength of the tide and the compromised integrity of her hull, led to *Princess Alice* listing

The scene of the disaster. © Illustrated London News/*Mary Evans Picture Library*

to port and breaking in two immediately in front of the paddle boxes. As *Bywell Castle* continued forward under her own momentum she knocked out the forward boiler and destroyed the forward saloon. In two minutes the severed bow section had foundered.

The stern section rose upwards and at 7:59pm, a mere four minutes after the collision, foundered in 18 feet of water. *Bywell Castle*, still affected by momentum, promptly ran over the wreckage, flattening the aft funnel and crushing the lifeboat davits. In the confusion of the sinking the two lifeboats were cut free by Long, but one capsized and most passengers had neither access nor time to use them. Some had been able to grab ropes thrown from *Bywell Castle*, or had climbed one of *Princess Alice's* funnels to *Bywell Castle's* deck, but her height meant most passengers were unable to do so. Through the rapid sinking there was no time for any emergency procedure, and there were no efficient means of evacuation. Those in the saloons had little chance of escape, there being only two survivors from below decks, while those above deck were flung into the river. They at least had a chance; based on the locations of bodies recovered and survivors' accounts the vast majority of survivors were on her open deck near the extreme bow or stern. Survivor accounts vary, but it appears that more men survived *Princess Alice* due to women's fashion of the day

hampering swimming – itself a skill few possessed. According to one account, Grinstead ordered a passenger to 'jump on a piece of the wreck' before crying:
    '*God Almighty - what is to be done?*'

The only damage *Bywell Castle* sustained was a bent hull plate and some scraped paint.

As soon as *Bywell Castle* struck *Princess Alice* Harrison ordered the lifeboats lowered. By the time they were launched the river was full of watermen who had seen the disaster, rescuing survivors. *Princess Alice's* sister ship *Duke of Teck* was among the rescue vessels. Thankfully, *Bywell Castle's* chief engineer, upon hearing the crash, ran up on deck and the order for full astern was not carried out, thus protecting those in the water from her exposed propeller. Some managed to swim ashore but according to one witness the river was 'covered with bonnets', and it was plain that there would be many fatalities. News of the disaster travelled quickly after the first survivors were brought ashore, but it was not until the next day that the police arrived; there being no formal alarm. Woolwich Harbourmaster Captain Fitzgerald was placed in charge of salvage and body recovery: watermen were paid two pounds per day to help the search and an additional 5 shillings for every body found, creating great interest in the work. Sheds at Woolwich Arsenal were requisitioned as mortuaries and Coroner Charles Carttar requested to begin the Coroner Inquests.

The bow section was salvaged almost immediately, 29 victims being recovered,

Recovering bodies from the wreck. © Illustrated London News/*Mary Evans Picture Library*

The severed bow of *Princess Alice* once salvaged. © Illustrated London News/*Mary Evans Picture Library*

and when the stern was beached on 8th September seven additional bodies were found. In total, it is believed over 800 were on board *Princess Alice*, with 640 lost. Even this latter figure is unreliable as some bodies may have floated down river, and several bodies recovered were possibly murder victims – the sinking enabling easy disposal. In the days that followed the area became so busy with sightseers that several minor accidents occurred on other pleasure steamers sailing to the wreck site. It was even found necessary to place a police guard around the beached wreck, as so many people were stealing 'souvenir' pieces of wood.

The public's desire for information about the disaster cannot be overestimated. *Princess Alice's* sinking was the first disaster to occur so close to Fleet Street, and the story ran continuously for over four months. The disaster was closely associated with two accidents which occurred just beforehand – the sinking of HMS *Eurydice* and the Sittingbourne railway crash. Ironically, Grinstead's brother (who also perished) had been hailed a hero for rescuing passengers from this railway accident.

The Press concentrated on survivors' accounts and Inquiry reports, but many letters were published suggesting safety improvements or placing perceived blame. Unfortunately these only added to the confusion and many inaccuracies were circulated. The most significant was an illustration in the *Illustrated London News* on 14th September. It showed *Princess Alice* being run down from astern – the exact opposite of what actually occurred. Due to this image, many believed *Bywell Castle* to be responsible and Harrison was nearly lynched after its publishing. In addition the log of *Bywell Castle* was published, leading to criticism by the London Steamboat Company because Grinstead 'cannot speak for himself', having drowned. Similarly there was another unfounded controversy. Only one 'runner' on *Bywell Castle* had been drunk, but he was not involved in the operation of the vessel. However, the whole crew was investigated because after the disaster he had gone to the nearest bar and repeatedly shouted 'It is the bloody booze', accusing everyone else aboard of being inebriated!

The survivors' accounts shocked society, particularly the number of children lost, yet there were some bittersweet endings. One off-duty police officer tried to save his wife, jumping overboard with her. He lost her for a moment before finding her hand again in the murky water. When they reached the shore, however, he found he had rescued a stranger – his wife had drowned. The lady he rescued had also lost her family, and

Bringing the dead ashore. © Illustrated London News/*Mary Evans Picture Library*

shortly afterwards they got married. Ironically, though, the most famous 'passenger' on *Princess Alice* never was on board. Elizabeth Stride, to become the third victim of 'Jack the Ripper', claimed her husband and two children were killed. She only survived by climbing up one of the ship's funnels from where she

was rescued. However, she never claimed from the Relief Fund, her husband is recorded as dying in 1884 and no 'Stride' is listed as lost. Plainly the story was invented to gain sympathy.

Many souvenirs were produced to raise funds, but the most long-term social repercussion was many Londoners starting to learn how to swim. A Mansion House relief fund was formed, raising £37,000 for those affected, but such was the feeling for those lost that 23,000 people donated sixpence towards a memorial to *Princess Alice's* dead, located even today by the mass graves of the unidentified in Woolwich Cemetery.

The first Inquiry was opened on 6th September 1878. It aimed to officially identify the cause of death of William Beachy, a stock-broker's clerk, who was the first victim identi-

Memorial to the *Princess Alice* victims, Woolwich Cemetery. *Author*

fied and thus chosen to represent all victims. Ultimately it was criticised for its length, principally due to Carttar's wish to identify the cause of the collision – not necessarily his jurisdiction – and for continually repetitive and irrelevant questioning. This became so farcical in public opinion that a derogatory song was written about it, with the lines:

> 'Oh, when will you stop, old man, they said,
> Oh, when will you stop, said they,
> When I've asked 50,000 more,
> Of the silliest Questions, hi hi.'

A Board of Trade Inquiry was subsequently held, beginning on 14th October and led by Thames Magistrate John Balguy. Along with the causes of the collision, the Inquiries investigated various other aspects. They questioned whether the passenger limits actually exceeded the vessel's design, particularly

considering the fragility of *Princess Alice*, but it was concluded that for a vessel of her size she was not overloaded. They did, however, consider a restriction on the number of passengers carried after dark. Equally there was criticism of the lack of any passenger manifest, especially as such a list would have assisted with the difficult task of identifying the dead, while lifeboat provision was also strongly faulted: *Princess Alice* having only two lifeboats and 12 life rings. The speed of the sinking,

Reading the names of the saved. © Illustrated London News/*Mary Evans Picture Library*

though, made this point academic.

Concerning the rapidity with which *Princess Alice* broke apart and sank, there was much debate over the strength and condition of her hull. Expert witnesses argued that she was far too fragile for Thames operation, providing a rotten plank from the wreck as evidence. The plank was later proved a fake, and the Inquiry concluded that no ship could have withstood the collision. Indeed, even after a week on the bottom the forward bulkheads were so solid that they had to be drilled in order to drain the forward saloon of water.

Naturally the primary issue investigated centred on the question of blame. The Inquiries found both ships equally culpable; both ship-owners contesting the verdict. As a result there was an Admiralty Court hearing, coming to the same conclusion, which was again contested by the owners of *Bywell Castle* in a Court of Appeal hearing in July 1879. Harrison was exonerated as the 'improper' final turn to port was deemed the only available option to try and avoid collision; blame ultimately being placed solely upon *Princess Alice*. In the process of coming to this conclusion, Long, Harrison and two engineers from *Bywell Castle* were accused of neglecting their duty, but were all found not guilty. Specific mention was made that Long's negligence in not keeping proper lookout did not contribute to the collision. While no-one was charged for their actions, Grinstead was allocated complete blame for the collision. Historians now though believe that the true fault lies with Eyres, having lost control of the vessel.

A die-cut 'In Memoriam' card for the *Princess Alice* victims. *Author's collection*

More broadly, serious concerns were revealed about shipping practices and the Thames itself. In addition to the multiple Inquiries and appeals, a separate 'Thames Traffic Committee' was established to investigate general practices and safety. The Port of London Authority was inspected regarding safety checks, their non-interference 'laissez-faire' policy revealed in their unwillingness to impose the unpopular and generally-ignored suggestion of following the international 'Rule of the Road'. Its need, and the dangers of 'laissez-faire' policy, were further emphasised by many earlier missed warnings. The worst (but not sole) example took place eleven years *prior* to *Princess Alice*, when another paddle steamer, *Metis*, was sunk by another collier, *Wentworth*, in exactly the same place for similar causes as in 1878. The sole reason that most survived this earlier accident was due to the helmsman's actions in beaching the forepart of the broken *Metis*.

As for the river, despite Carttar passing a verdict of 'death by drowning' the condition of Thames water raised serious doubts, particularly due to the location of the sinking – between the outflows of Joseph Bazelgette's new sewage system. Built as a consequence of the 'Great Stink' when the condition of the Thames in central London became too foul to bear, it was a positive start but only moved the problem further down-river – the untreated contents being released at Woolwich. That day, all of London's sewers had been emptied shortly before the accident occurred. Investigated in great detail, chemists were called as expert witnesses who argued that the decomposing sewage in the Thames released 'sulphuretted hydrogen' (the cause of the 'stink'). Now known as hydrogen sulphide, this poisonous, corrosive, flammable, and explosive chemical was created by the breakdown of organic matter without oxygen, notably occurring in sewers. Five minutes in such polluted water was deemed sufficient to fatally poison:

> *'According to the evidence of survivors, the water – rather let's call it the liquid – swallowed by those immersed was absolutely poisonous.'*

> *'At high water* [ebb tides], *twice in twenty-four hours, the flood gates of the*

Identifying the dead at Woolwich. © Illustrated London News/*Mary Evans Picture Library*

> *outfalls are opened when there is projected into the river two continuous columns*
> *of decomposed fermenting sewage, hissing like soda water with baneful gasses,*
> *so black that the water is stained for miles and discharging a corrupt charnel*
> *house odour that will be remembered by all who have passed through it on these*
> *summer excursions as being peculiarly depressing and sickening.'*

Considering the numbers who mentioned this in the Inquiries and the purportedly large number of survivors who rapidly died after the disaster (not included in the death toll), many now consider that those who died were poisoned before they were able to drown. The exceptionally warm summer, pollution and lack of refrigeration made decomposition occur much faster than expected, with complaints of the smell emanating from the temporary mortuary at Woolwich Arsenal. Identification of victims, therefore, became all the more unpleasant, to the point that the Police ordered to guard the beached wreckage nearby were issued smelling salts. Due to these issues the Metropolitan Board of Works was coerced to investigate the cleanliness of the Thames, but later declared it safe! Pollution continued to be an issue in the ensuing decades and it was only by the 1950s that major improvements began to be seen. Today the Thames is one of the cleanest rivers in the world.

The principal recommendations arising from the *Princess Alice* Disaster were to impose speed limits, place rules on how vessels of different types were to pass each other and enforce the port-to-port 'Rule of the Road'. Today Britain is still the only country which stipulates this on navigable rivers. There were suggestions about updating lifeboat regulations, while the Thames Police were later provided with steam launches to enable faster response times. It was also suggested that future steamers should have the wheel forward of the first funnel to aid visibility.

In the aftermath of the disaster Harrison suffered a breakdown and never sailed again. *Bywell Castle* disappeared off the Bay of Biscay in 1883 due to being overloaded in a gale, while the London Steamboat Company filed for bankruptcy in 1884. As for *Princess Alice* herself, she was taken to Greenwich for scrapping; her engines salvaged and fitted into a new vessel. Diminishing in people's memory, the disaster became all but forgotten as a feeling of safety returned to the Thames, in spite of some locals renaming Galleon's Reach 'Haunted Reach'. This remained until a similar disaster in 1989 brought safety on the Thames into question again – the *Marchioness*.

Today, *Marchioness* still makes news while *Princess Alice* is largely forgotten. Nonetheless, the sinking of *Princess Alice* had caused shockwaves nationwide. This was the first major publicised disaster on the Thames, and many minor accidents reported within days after the disaster highlighted how dangerous the crowded River Thames was. With the possible exception of HMS *Royal George* in 1782, she remains the worst disaster to have occurred in British waters, and the legacy of the 'Rule of the Road' continues to this day. But there is a valid warning for the future. Considering that *Princess Alice* and, over a hundred years later, *Marchioness* foundered in very similar circumstances – on a comparatively empty river after elsewise-avoidable collisions – it would appear that some questions of safety still remain unanswered, and some of the lessons of history are still to be learnt. It can only be hoped that there will never be a repetition…

Relatives seeking news. © Illustrated London News/*Mary Evans Picture Library*

ON A 'WING' AND A PRAYER
The British Imperial Airship Scheme 1924–30

In aviation history there have been many infamous events: the disappearance of Amelia Earhart, the De Havilland Comet tragedies, the destruction of the *Hindenburg*. But there is one event of major significance that very few people appear to have heard of which was at one point Britain's most publicised engineering project – the British Imperial Airship Scheme of 1924, and His Majesty's Airships *R100* and *R101*.

The development of the 'airship' owes its origins to Graf Ferdinand von Zeppelin and the ground-breaking *LZ1* of 1900. Today, 'airship' and 'Zeppelin' are synonymous terms but really they were no such thing, the latter solely applying to airships built by the Zeppelin Company of Friedrichshafen. Furthermore, the term 'airship', or more technically 'dirigible' (from the French for 'directable'), is itself a generic name encompassing three different types of airframe. Most common today are non-rigid designs or blimps, whereby the external shape is maintained solely by gas pressure. Second are semi-rigid airships. Although mostly dependent on gas pressure, these have a structural keel for rigidity. Lastly were the famous rigid airships. These consisted of a linen-

R101 riding at the mooring mast with the Cardington Sheds in the background. *Author's collection*

clad framework often made of steel or an aluminium alloy dubbed 'duralumin', inside of which were multiple gasbags. It was this rigid design that the 'R' in later British airship names stood for.

British rigid airship construction began with His Majesty's Airship *No.1* (also known as *Mayfly*), completed in 1911 in direct competition with Germany. Never flown, a handling error when being taken out of her shed (airship terminology never using the word 'hangar') caused the delicate structure to snap. Lessons were learnt though and many rigid and non-rigid ships were constructed and tested, culminating in the *R33* of 1919. Converted for civilian use in 1920 but later returned to military duty as an experimental flying aircraft carrier, she ultimately had a ten-year career. Her sister *R34* became the first airship to cross the Atlantic.

These vessels – as with all airships – had limitations, being particularly vulnerable to storms and shifting winds placing stress on their frames. The use of hydrogen furthered the danger; sparks from engines and static a constant fear. Production in sufficient quantities of the safer helium only began in America in 1921, but they refused to sell to other nations for fear it would be used for military purposes.

These dangers were dramatically demonstrated on 24th August 1921. America had purchased the part-built *R38* from the British Government in 1919. Completed in early 1921, it was to be tested with an Anglo-American crew before being handed over to the American Navy as the *ZR-2*. Found to have design problems, on her fifth flight while flying in fair weather offshore near Hull she suffered a complete structural failure, snapping in two. As she fell the forward section exploded and the wreck crashed into the Humber, killing 44. Citing financial reasons the British Government had already cancelled airship development on 31st May 1921, and with this high profile incident it was thought the British construction of airships had come to an end.

But not for long…

By July 1921 there was already discussion about re-instigating an airship programme, the Agent-General for Tasmania, A.H. Ashbolt, first proposing an imperial airship company. Stalling, in 1922 Dennistoun Burney from the Vickers Company, which had built many early British airships, suggested a commercial British Empire passenger service. Looked at favourably, this idea lingered until the 1924 General Election: a minority win by Ramsay Macdonald and Labour. Their new Minister of Air, Lord Thomson, credited the plan as feasible but financially problematic as it depended on Government loans, potentially requiring sixty years to pay back. Instead he proposed a new Government scheme intended to last for three years and cost £1,200,000 – the Imperial Airship Scheme.

Forming two advisory bodies, it would operate a series of intended routes across Canada, Africa, India and Australia, notably creating major overseas airship stations at Montreal and Karachi. Most importantly, the question of funding numerous airships was resolved by initiating a revolutionary competition. Initially there were to be two ships – one built by the Government and another by private enterprise.

Some words are necessary on Lord Thomson. Born in India in 1875 to a military family, he became an officer in the Royal Engineers and served in the second Boer War, during which he was placed to a balloon section – triggering a great interest in aviation. Leaving the army after World War One he entered politics, but despite standing as a Labour candidate three times failed to win a seat. Ramsay Macdonald, however, wanted Thompson on his cabinet, therefore had him elevated to the peerage as Baron Thomson of Cardington, Bedfordshire. Strate-

Lord Thomson. © *Illustrated London News/Mary Evans Picture Library*

gically, this was the site of the Government's airship works. Taking the position of Secretary of State for Air, the 1924 minority Government collapsed after eleven months, being replaced by Stanley Baldwin's conservative cabinet. It was only in the 1929 election that Macdonald returned with his second minority administration and Thomson was again made Secretary of State for Air.

As noted, two ships were to be constructed; one privately and one publicly. Designated *R100* and *R101*, they were quickly nicknamed the 'capitalist ship' and the 'socialist ship'. While of radically different designs each was ordered to fit the same specifications: passenger accommodation for 100, capacity for 16 tons of cargo and to carry fuel sufficient for fifty-seven hours flight at a cruising speed of 63mph. Their final acceptance into passenger service was dependant on completing test flights to India.

R100 was designed and built by the Airship Guarantee Company – a dedicated subsidiary of the Vickers Company in Howden, Yorkshire. Although planning began immediately, delays meant construction only commenced in 1927 and the fixed cost laid out by the Government, £471,113, meant the construction project was expect to make a loss right from the start. Therefore she was designed to use as few machine tools and as few different components as possible, while her construction shed was unheated and leaked, in part leading to a number of strikes throughout construction.

Her chief designer was an experienced airship engineer who would ultimately become a household name for very different aeronautics – Barnes Wallis of WWII 'bouncing bomb' fame. Another noteworthy designer was novelist Neville Shute Norway.

With a length of 719 feet and a diameter of 133 feet, *R100* had the volume capacity for five million cubic feet of hydrogen. Weighing 105 tons empty, with

R100 at Saint-Hubert Aerodrome, near Montreal, August 1930. *(Author's collection)*

a total lift of 150 tons, she could carry a payload of ballast, fuel, passengers and cargo weighing 45 tons. Her main structure consisted of 16 longitudinal girders formed from duralumin tubes running between 15 polygonal transverse frames. The 15 gasbags used a revolutionary new geodetic wire bracing design by Wallis that would later inspire the airframe fuselages in his WWII bombers. Forming the outer hull or 'envelope' was a cover of linen fabric painted with aluminium aircraft dope.

In terms of propulsion, plans changed several times throughout construction – itself a stop-start affair as it closely followed each stage of the designing process. Originally she was to have engines fuelled by hydrogen and kerosene but these were insufficiently developed, while proposed diesel engines were too heavy and unreliable. Instead, Wallis decided to use six modified Rolls-Royce Condor aero engines. Fuelled by petrol (and requiring a greater volume), this was considered a fire risk in tropical conditions, leading to the final test route being changed to Canada instead of India. The engines were fitted in three gondolas, two apiece, with the rear 'pusher' engines fitted with reversing gears for docking.

While meant to be a 'traditional' design, Wallis made much of *R100* quite experimental. Aside from her structure and wiring, her physical shape was the first properly aerodynamic airship and the first with

Period postcard of the passenger viewing balcony, R100. *Author's collection*

internal passenger accommodation. Wallis also devised a number of additional operating systems, such as rainwater collection devices along the top of the ship to restock ballast en-route.

In terms of passenger accommodation, entry to the ship was via a doorway in the bow leading to an electrically-lit corridor. Slightly forward of centre inside the hull was an enclosed three-storey structure comprising an upper deck with cabins, lounge balcony and promenade balconies; main deck with kitchen, dining room, conveniences, promenades and further cabins; and the crew deck containing their accommodation. Beneath this externally was the control gondola from where the airship was operated. With panoramic windows for the promenades and a double staircase, the passenger provisions were an unusual blend of spartan and luxury – the result of balancing amenities provided versus incumbent weight. *R100* was ultimately described as 'intermediate in comfort between a Pullman train and an ocean liner'.

It was only by 1929 that *R100* was completed, having taken three years. Her first flight took place on 16th December 1929 from Howden via York to Cardington. Running with one failed engine, the journey took five hours forty-seven minutes. The next day she undertook a six and a half hour trial. This would have been a flight to London, however, a section of covering detached from the lower fin so instead they flew around Cardington. She was shedded and her cover wiring examined over December. By the end of January 1930 *R100* had completed five flights, including a fifty-four hour flight over South East England. She had also achieved a personal best speed of 81.5mph. At this point she was given new upgraded Condor engines and a few cabins were removed to reduce weight. Her return to flight was delayed by a gust damaging her tail, unfortunately timed as it occurred when the German airship *Graf Zeppelin* was visiting England, so limiting publicity and denying a ride to famed designer Dr Hugo Eckener of the Zeppelin Company. It had been planned to have her maiden voyage to Canada on the 25th, but her repair test flight on 21st May led to the tapered tail breaking. It was thus removed, reducing her length to 709 feet. With a further test flight to check repairs, her maiden voyage was finalised for late July and she was officially handed over to the Air Ministry.

At 2:48am, 29th July 1930, *R100* departed Cardington bound for Montreal. Her commander was Squadron Leader Ralph Booth, in command of a collective crew of 36. Outward bound there were only six passengers, including Wing Commander Reginald Colmore, Director of Airship Development and Major George Scott, Superintendent of Flying Operations. All was well until the next day, when a sudden squall caused damage to the fins and repairs had to be made mid-flight. A large storm was forecast over the St Lawrence River, but Major Scott directed that they should fly straight through it. Despite *R100* never having been tested in adverse weather, Booth complied. Shortly afterwards a blast of wind forced the airship upwards 1800 feet in a single minute, before another gust lifted them another thousand in barely fifteen seconds – some 45mph vertically. Trying to combat the ascents *R100's* elevators were lowered, causing the airship to tilt steeply downwards. As rapidly as it had begun she returned to an even keel and was soon out of the storm, bearing a massive tear to the lower side of the starboard fin. Nonetheless, she arrived safely in Montreal at 5:37am, having travelled 3364 miles in seventy-eight hours, forty-nine minutes.

Despite continuing teething troubles the voyage was seen as a triumph. The crew were invited to receptions and banquets, while *R100* undertook a twenty-six hour 'local' flight to Quebec with officials. She was a sensation, having over 100,000 visitors *daily* over her twelve-day stay.

She departed for home on 13th August, loaded with 13 passengers including nine journalists. With one engine out of action and water ingress shorting the electric cooker the three-day return journey was not the most comfortable, but there were no major difficulties and she arrived at Cardington on 16th August. Thereafter, she was shedded for inspection as attention turned to her sister. She had travelled 11,135 miles in ten

Period postcard of the main passenger staircase, R100. *Author's collection*

flights, with a total flying time of 294 hours ten minutes. Circumstances would mean she would never fly again.

R100 was not a glowing success. Aside from teething troubles, her outer cover was barely adequate – insufficiently supported, it rippled badly in flight, increasing the chances of tearing. Her speed was thus limited to 70mph. By the time she returned from Canada her cover and gasbags were life-expired. Then there was the snapped tail. Most fundamentally, she failed to meet the requirements of the project: she was slightly too heavy and with underpowered engines, reducing her lift and thus potential payload to below the minimum stipulated. Furthermore, weight had been saved to an extent by the use of petrol engines despite diesels being stipulated – preventing Indian usage.

But it would be unfair to criticise too harshly. What Wallis built, by his own admission, was a prototype with the aim of learning from experiment. *R100* would never have realistically made a commercial service; she was simply there to pave the way. To her credit, she more than compensated with her impressive speed, even if her maximum caused the cover to ripple excessively. Excluding the storm, her flights were relatively free from incident. Therefore, despite her flaws, *R100* and Barnes Wallis deserve praise for what they achieved.

Although *R100* had been built in Howden, she was ultimately based at Cardington, near Bedford. The establishment here was originally built by the

The Cardington Sheds, 2010 (Shed 1 for R101 on the left, Shed 2 for R100 on the right). *Author*

Short Brothers Company in 1915, comprising Shed No. 1, construction workshops, a gas works supplying hydrogen and the workers housing estate named Shortstown. Nationalised in 1919 and renamed the Royal Airship Works, it was mothballed in 1921. Many modifications were made to the site for the Imperial Airship Scheme, including extending Shed 1, erecting Shed 2 – formerly at Pulham air base – and constructing a new mooring mast. Costing £50,000, this mast was 202 feet tall and featured a spiral staircase, lift, winches and underground fuel tanks. Similar masts were built at Montreal, at Ismailia in Egypt and at the Indian terminus at Karachi.

The developments at Cardington made it the national centre for lighter than air travel. Today all that remains are the great sheds, still dominating the skyline. 812 feet long, 180 feet wide and 157 feet tall, they are so big that clouds have been known to form inside them. As a scale comparison, the ocean liners *Lusitania* and *Mauretania* could be placed together inside each shed, while only 70 feet of *Titanic's* bow would protrude past the doors.

R101 started life at Cardington, being built in Shed 1, and developed very differently. Unlike the fixed cost given to Vickers, the Government lavished resources on 'their' airship with the final construction cost reaching £711,595 – over half as much again as *R100*. The first two years consisted solely of research,

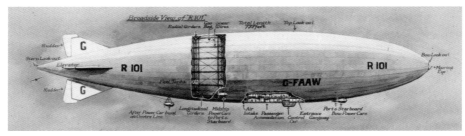

Diagram of R101. © Illustrated London News/*Mary Evans Picture Library*

costing £305,200 alone. This included stress calculations, and designing and testing new machinery and materials, in addition to the actual structural design work. They even constructed an entire bay purely to research in-flight stresses – it being subsequently dismantled and tested to destruction. The mothballed *R33* was used as test-bed for the project, adding a further £103,100 to the scheme's cost.

R101 Designer, Vincent Richmond. © Illustrated London News/*Mary Evans Picture Library*

Leading the design team was Lieutenant-Colonel Vincent Richmond, who had helped devise the criteria for the scheme and was experienced with airships, albeit mostly non-rigid designs. Some claimed ever-growing rivalry between the two competing groups hindering development, others strongly denying this, but the fundamental issue was that Britain barely had the expertise to build one airship of this nature, let alone two. Neville Shute Norway of *R100* later recounted that he was 'inexpressibly shocked' that the *R101* design team was essentially the same as that for the ill-fated *R38*…

Measuring 735 feet long with a diameter of 131 feet, *R101's* design was indeed revolutionary. For additional strength her structure was primarily made from stainless steel, with lesser use of duralumin. The girders were designed and built by Boulton & Paul in Norwich and transported to Cardington where they were bolted together. She was made up of 20 transverse ring frames with 15 connecting longitudinal girders, but unlike previous airships these rings were entirely self-supporting. Being thicker overall as a result, however, they reduced the size of the 16 gasbags. Her cover was equally radical, Richmond experimenting with fitting pre-doped linen. His enthusiasm towards perfecting this process led to him being given the nickname of 'Dope'.

Originally *R101* had a total weight of 113 tons and a total lift of 148 tons. This only gave 35 tons of useful lift, as opposed to the 63 tons required, and when removing the 'serving load' of 18 tons of ballast, this resulted in a maximum payload of only 17 tons (including fuel). A major issue, this

The framing of R101 with cylindrical fuel tanks and one gas bag in situ. © Illustrated London News/*Mary Evans Picture Library*

Top: A surviving R101 Beardmore Tornado aero engine. *Author with permission from the Science Museum, London*

Above: Diagram of a two-berth cabin aboard R101. © *Illustrated London News/Mary Evans Picture Library*

would return to haunt the project.

Whereas *R100* had turned to petrol engines against the stipulated requirements, *R101* used the diesels intended for the purpose. Having five Beardmore Tornado aero engines, these were positioned two each side and one aft centrally. 450rpm slower and collectively six tons heavier than intended, these were developed for *R101* by doubling up pre-existing railway engine designs. Ironically, all bar one retained a small petrol starter engine. They were prone to vibration that destroyed the original reversible propellers, these being replaced with fixed wooden props, forcing the forward port engine propeller to be fitted backwards to enable reverse. This astonished the *R100* designers, and later two engines were modified to run in reverse when necessary.

Turning to passenger accommodation, *R101* was intended to be as luxurious as possible, but the overall layout changed substantially through the design phase and with later modifications. Having two decks, the uppermost contained passenger accommodation, lounge, dining room and promenades. The lower deck housed washrooms, galley, crew's quarters, cargo hold and the first ever airship smoking room – asbestos lined to be fireproof. As with *R100*, there was an external control gondola and passenger boarding access via a corridor from the bow. Much was done to save weight: walls were white-painted canvas, pillars were hollow around structural members and most furniture was wickerwork with inflatable cushions. Quoting one reporter: 'The *R101* will provide luxuries undreamt of by Jules Verne and H.G. Wells. It will positively be an aerial hotel.'

R101 was full of innovations. Lacking frame braces, a new method of gasbag suspension was devised; a net supporting the bag akin to parachute wiring.

Passenger promenade area on R101.
© Illustrated London News/*Mary Evans Picture Library*

Above left: The scale of R101: three quarters of a propeller, damaged after striking the mooring mast.
Author with permission from The Shuttleworth Collection

Above right: Passenger Lounge aboard R101. © Illustrated London News/*Mary Evans Picture Library*

New automatic gas relief valves were designed, fitted either side of each bag, with vents at the bow preventing any build-up of gas internally by allowing a continual flow of air. Ballast and fuel tanks were linked via a compressed air system, allowing trimming of the vessel when in flight, while the fuel tanks were designed to be jettisoned in an emergency. The rudders and elevator controls were assisted by servo gear, while miniature propellers drove electric generators when in flight. These and other ideas though, were utterly untested. For good and bad, *R101* was truly revolutionary.

She was finally completed in 1929, behind schedule. This was after Labour returned to power so Thomson did not miss out on the test flights, and he was particularly keen to publicise 'his' ship. On 14th October 1929 *R101* first took to

Period postcard of R101 flying over St Paul's Cathedral, one example of the publicity surrounding the airship.

Author's collection

W & K London.   R101 THE WORLD'S LARGEST AIRSHIP   No 19 9.
OVER LONDON.

Period postcard of R101 at the mooring mast. *Author's collection*

the skies, undertaking a return flight over London, albeit on only two engines. Even before this flight it was known the weight problem would prevent a passage to India. While working out a solution tests were continued, her second flight on 18th October over the Midlands lasting nine hours thirty-eight minutes. A success, it was only marred by Scott insisting on mooring the airship himself and messing it up twice – dumping too much ballast, so throwing her trim, then overshooting the mast and tangling mooring lines. Nonetheless, Thompson declared to the Press: *'I have rarely had a more pleasant experience. There is a feeling of complete detachment and security…'*

Over November she undertook five flights across England, notably over the Norwich works of Boulton & Paul where her girders had been made. Varying in duration and with engine difficulties, many of these flights carried dignitaries, while a lunch for 100 MPs was held on board on the 23rd. Her fastest run in this period was 67.5mph.

The last November flight was on the 18th – an endurance test to last at least thirty-six hours. Flying 1148 miles over Scotland, Ireland and the Midlands, it actually lasted thirty hours forty-one minutes. Shortly afterwards she disappeared from public view for a major refit, lasting from 30th November 1929 to 23rd June 1930. Desperate to increase lift, 12 passenger cabins, two lavatories, two ballast tanks, her servo gear and all promenade window glass were removed, the lattermost replaced with 'Cellon' cellulose. Most importantly, the wiring holding the gasbags in place was slackened, allowing the bags to swell with more hydrogen.

On 26th June 1930 she returned to test flights, the following two days having involvement in the prestigious RAF Display at Hendon. Thomson had achieved spectacular publicity – the test flights being for 'public relations' as much as engineering, in some cases more so. Over a million people descended on

Cardington to watch her from the road. Throughout construction each new technological advance was heralded in the Press, making it awkward to remove later. Coupled with the limitations placed on Richmond by the specifications, the publicity began to be a hindrance – expectations were constantly being raised.

The Press were besotted. Indeed, *R101* was a beautiful ship, but it was rapidly found that, unfortunately, she flew like a pig. Many unexpected difficulties arose, all of them major. After the *R38* disaster the Government had feared another structural failure so created strict parameters for design. It was partly under this that Richmond used self-supporting transverse frames – increasing weight and decreasing gasbag size, limiting potential lift. Then the engines were overweight, underpowered and unreliable. It would have been logical to remove them, but as the Government's ship they were not in a position to ignore the Government's requirements, especially as Richmond had helped create them.

As outlined, modifications were thus made to lighten the airship, notably expanding the gasbags. But this had consequences of its own. It was found that the bags increasingly surged back and forth inside the hull, reducing stability even when stationary. The relief valves were found to be very sensitive and leaked gas, the surging hindering the issue further. Worse yet, the bags rubbed against the frames – again increasing with the surging. With some 4000 protruding bolts, holes were worn in the fabric and even more gas leaked, further reducing lift.

Collectively these issues all made controlling her ever more difficult. For example, while at Hendon *R101* was seen by 150,000 people, who were highly impressed when she dipped her bow in salute to the King. But this triggered a sudden crash dive – falling 500ft – and she only recovered due to the quick actions of the Coxswain. On the previous flight she had even been forced to dump 2 tons of fuel, to the chagrin of the farmer below.

Clearly in need of desperate measures, those already completed were not the only ones planned, entering the shed again from 29th June until 1st October 1930. To mitigate chafing, 4,000 'cushions' were fitted to exposed frame areas and the gasbags overhauled. Two engines were also made reversible at this point. But the biggest job, delayed from December 1929, was the most radical modification possible. Urgently needing lift and running out of things to remove, they cut *R101* in half. Once severed, a new gasbag and bay was assembled amidships, bringing her volume up to 5,509,753 cubic feet of hydrogen. Increased in length to 777 feet, *R101* still remains the largest

R101 in flight. *Author's collection*

aircraft ever built in Britain. Having an increased weight of 118 tons versus an increased lift of 167 tons, she produced 49 tons of useful lift – 14 tons more than before. Finally she could get to India, on paper at least.

While this may all sound very unhealthy, unbelievably there was an even bigger problem. Fitted pre-doped, despite testing *R101's* cover was found to suffer from humidity, tearing when fitted and splitting even before she first left the shed. An inspection on 20th January 1930 revealed that by then some areas had actually begun to rot. To repair this, reinforcement bands were glued in place along her length, but this backfired spectacularly. Neville Shute Norway of *R100* was shown a piece; in his own words:

> *'It was ordinary outer cover, linen fabric, silver doped in a red oxide base. On the inner surface two-inch tapes had been stuck with some adhesive, evidently for strengthening. I didn't know what I was expected to say, and turned it about in my hands, and suddenly my hand went through it. In parts it was friable, like scorched brown paper, so that if you crumpled it in your hand it broke up into flakes. I stared at it in horror thinking of R100.'*
>
> *'Good God. Where did that come off?'*

He was told by Booth:

> *'All right. That's not off our ship. That's off R101.'*

Norway simply replied:

> *'I hope they have got all this stuff off the ship.'*

This fault massively reduced the strength of the fabric – the rubber glue having reacted with the dope. An inspection on 2nd June found many tears developing, so it was decided to replace this pre-doped cover with a new one doped afterwards in the traditional way. But this was only to be done after the Hendon flights. In the meantime, it was reinforced further. This plainly did not help as the cover tore twice more, the largest being by 140 feet. Patched again with yet more strengthening bands, when she was extended in length the cover was finally replaced. *Almost.* Two areas which had been originally been fitted before doping were deemed acceptable – just forward of the fins and wrapping around the bow. These

Bow of R101 (note the differing colour shades of the outer cover – evidence for the different types of repair carried out). ©Illustrated London News/*Mary Evans Picture Library*

areas had also been reinforced with glue strips before realising the problem this caused, but as there was no time left to replace them they were strengthened by patching another layer over them.

The reason for suddenly-diminishing time was an unofficial deadline – 4th October 1930. Thompson had said that he would defer to the experts on when they thought she would be ready for a long-distance flight; to quote him before the House of Lords in June 1930:

'There is going to be no risk while I am in charge. No lives will be sacrificed through lack of foresight and skill.'

With the maiden flight delayed from late September as it was, a number of circumstances would ultimately lead to those very risks. First was the successful Canadian flight of *R100* in July 1930. With Thompson publicising *R101* as the more revolutionary, building expectations, the designers could not back down and say she was inferior – they had to show what public money had bought. Then there was a planned Imperial Conference in October-November 1930. As a project specifically dealing with communication across the Empire, Thompson was adamant that the flight take place so he could report news of the success. Lastly, and no doubt linked through a desire to show his own personal capabilities, Thompson had been asked in private by Prime Minister Macdonald to consider being the next Viceroy of India.

Had there been no pressure on the builders it is unlikely she would have flown, but in fairness it is doubtful Thompson was told of all the risks; the designers keeping him in the dark. It may be for this reason that despite poor lift he requested a 2630 square foot blue Axminster carpet be fitted in the entrance gangway and lounge – over half a ton of it. In his mind, the time for testing was past: he needed *R101* operational and immediately.

After all the modifications made, most particularly the new cover and extended length, *R101* was effectively an untested new airship, so one final trial was squeezed in overnight from 1st October. Lasting sixteen hours fifty-one minutes, despite perfect weather a faulty engine meant she could not be tested

A near-broadside view of R101. © Illustrated London News/*Mary Evans Picture Library*

at full speed. By this point she had flown a total of 3970 miles in 119 hours, forty-seven minutes.

Interestingly, the new 'Air Member for Supply and Research', Hugh Dowding (later of Fighter Command fame) was a passenger on this flight. Trusting the advice of Director Colmore, Dowding recommended a full speed trial be undertaken early in the maiden voyage itself, rather than delay it. He was – in his own words – 'responsible for the decision that a special flight for the purpose should not be carried out.'

On 4th October 1930, *R101* was scheduled to depart. Her route comprised two halves: Bedford to Ismalia, taking a course over Toulouse and Malta, and once refuelled on to Karachi. She was loaded with provisions and luggage, including a cask of ale, two cases of champagne, approximately 22lbs of luggage per passenger and, by request of Thomson for use at state dinners in Karachi, *another* carpet. To shorten refuelling in Ismailia there was also an additional nine tons of diesel fuel. It should be remembered that lift was still such an issue that purportedly biscuits had been removed from tins and parachutes left behind to save weight.

Her complement on this maiden voyage was six passengers and 48 crew – 54 in total. The dignitaries were important figures in aviation, especially airships:

Thomson and his valet James Buck, Director of Civil Aviation Air Vice Marshall Sir William Sefton Brancker, Chief Inspector with the Air Inspectorate Department Major Percy Bishop, Squadron Leader Palstra representing the Australian Government and Deputy Director of Civil Aviation, India Squadron Leader O'Neill.

The remainder comprised 30 hands, seven petty officers and 11 Royal Airship Works officials. Six officials technically did not have crew roles: Director Colmore, Major Scott, designers Richmond and Squadron Leader Michael Rope, Alexander Bushfield (also with the Aeronautical Inspection Department) and Harry

Ernest Johnston (navigator), Sir Sefton Brancker, Lord Tompson and Vincent Richmond preparing to board R101. © *Illustrated London News/Mary Evans Picture Library*

Leech, a Foreman Engineer at Cardington.

Of the working crew, some 42, the most significant were her officers: Squadron Leader Ernest Johnston as Navigator, Lieutenant-Commander Noel Atherstone as First Officer, Flying Officer Maurice Steff as Second Officer, Maurice Giblett as Chief Meteorological Officer, George 'Sky' Hunt as Chief

Coxswain, William Gent as Chief Engineer and Spencer Keeley as Chief Wireless Operator.

Her captain was Flight Lieutenant Herbert Carmichael Irwin. He was very experienced and a seasoned flyer, commanding the *R33*, *R36* and *R80* amongst others. As such, he gained the nickname 'Bird'. Aged thirty-six, he participated in the 1920 Summer Olympics in cross-country running; his former club still has the 'Irwin Memorial Challenge Cup'.

The crew had flown with each other in the past and throughout the trials, and were all apprehensive of the trip – a fear apparently justified by the circumstances of her leaving. Under her trials *R101* had been given temporary 'Permits to Fly' by Sefton Brancker. On 3rd July Inspector McWade had written directly to the Director of Aeronautical Inspection wishing to rescind even these temporary permits, fearing the results of expanding the gasbags – particularly the effectiveness of the padding in preventing holes. Director Outram knew little of airships so queried it with Airship Director Colmore, who unsurprisingly played the matter down. *R101* was ultimately given her 'Certificate of Airworthiness', but it is telling that despite being signed on 2nd October, Irwin only received the finalised copy on the very day she departed.

First Officer Atherstone's diary aptly summarised the crew's thoughts both on certification and the pressures they were put under with the tests:

> *'All these window-dressing stunts and joy-rides before she has got an Airworthiness Certificate are quite wrong, but there is no-one in the RAW* [Royal Airship Works] *executive who has got the guts to put their foot down and insist on trials being free of joy-rides.'*

The day before departure, he wrote:

> *'Everybody is rather keyed up now, as we all feel that the future of airships very largely depends on what sort of show we put up. There are very many unknown factors and I feel that that thing called 'Luck' will figure rather conspicuously in our flight. Let's hope for good luck and do our best…'*

Thomson, however, optimistically declared shortly before boarding:

> *'She is as safe as a house—except for the millionth chance.'*

At 6:36pm, 4th October 1930, *R101* began her maiden voyage. Dropping four tons of ballast immediately, she circled Bedford before heading south. Forecasts had not been good; it was raining and getting worse. Already she was pitching slightly, no doubt affecting her gas valves. More disconcerting was the initial altitude of barely 600ft and speed of only 35mph, with one engine playing up yet again, but by 8:21pm when over London they were stable at 1500 feet. Messaging to Cardington their intention to head towards Paris, there was no turning back. Around 10:00pm when over the Channel she dropped to circa 750 feet; Atherstone took over from the Height Coxswain and ordered that she not go under 1000 feet. Taking two hours to cross the Channel, the faulty engine being restarted, at 11.36pm she reported:

'Crossing French coast at Pointe de St Quentin. Wind 245 true. 35mph.'

The weather had deteriorated badly with low clouds, rain and south-westerly winds up to 50 mph. Working at top cruising speed, 63mph, the wind reduced her actual ground speed by half and blew her off course to the east. This was her first time at full speed since her refit, and she had never flown in stormy conditions before.

Still 15 miles off-course at about 1:00am, *R101* passed over the hilltop town of Poix-de-Picardie before turning on a new path. This would cross over the 770 foot Beauvais Ridge – an area known for unpredictable turbulence. At 1:51am Le Bourget wireless station reported her position was near Beauvais. An acknowledgement received at 1:52am was the last message from *R101*. Changing shift at 2:00am, Second Officer Steff and Coxswain Hunt took over. Battling the storm, progress was slow at only 20mph as they passed Allonne village.

At 2:06am her bow began dipping, ballast being dropped. One minute later she suddenly fell into a steep dive, throwing people and furniture off-balance. In ninety seconds she fell 500 feet as Hunt pulled the elevators hard up and dumped more ballast. At 2:08am she was back level but still descending at 290 feet per minute. At an altitude of 530 feet, a height not even *R101's* length, the engines were slowed. With her nose only three degrees up despite the elevators, those in command knew it was all over. Coxswain Hunt left the gondola, running through the crew's quarters shouting *'We're down, lads.'* After thirty seconds *R101* dived again, and with a rigger releasing the forward emergency ballast bags, at 2:09am she hit the ground – a wood 2.5 miles southwest of Beauvais. Travelling at

A night-time departure for R101 visually similar to her final flight.
© Illustrated London News/*Mary Evans Picture Library*

The morning after: the skeleton of R101. © *Illustrated London News/Mary Evans Picture Library*

13.8mph, at an angle around 18 degrees, it was an almost perfect emergency landing. Although her bow collapsed on impact and the forward starboard engine twisted around, this was not a violent landing; she bounced for 60 feet but the groove dug in the ground by her nosecone was scarcely nine feet long. But sadly it was not over. With leaking gasbags mixing with air, 5,509,753 cubic feet of hydrogen detonated. The 'millionth chance' had happened.

Only one person witnessed the disaster, Eugene Rabouile, who was hunting rabbits:

'I clearly saw the passengers' quarters, well-lit, and the green and red lights on the right and left of the airship. Suddenly there was a violent squall. The airship dipped by the nose several times, and its forepart crashed into the northwest edge of the Bois des Coutumes. There was at once a tremendous explosion, which knocked me down.

Soon flames rose into the sky to a great height – perhaps 300 feet. Everything was enveloped by them. I saw human figures running about like madmen in the wreck. Then I lost my head and ran away into the woods.'

Most survivors came from the engine cars, water ballast tanks soaking them as they scrambled free. Foreman Leech from Cardington had been in the smoking room, only escaping by hacking a hole in the wall and jumping through

The wreck of R101. © *Illustrated London News/Mary Evans Picture Library*

the side of the hull. He landed in a tree where, in his words, the rain 'cooled me off'. Wireless Operator Disley, woken by Hunt, attempted to cut the electrics during the second dive but failed, before he too had to claw out of the burning hulk. Eight people got clear of the flames, two of whom later died. According to legend Hunt also got clear, but on seeing that his friend Wally Potter was missing returned to the conflagration. Neither survived.

The six who returned home were: Arthur Bell, John Binks, Alfred Cook, Arthur Disley, Harry Leech, and Victor Savory. 48 had been killed. Only 26 bodies could be identified, 21 from dental records. Thomson was never identified.

At 3:16am, Le Bourget wireless station sent the brief message 'GFAAW a pris feu' – *R101* caught fire. Previously Disley had run to a phone, informing the Air Ministry 'she's gone up in flames'. Illuminating the night sky, broken and

Coffins aboard HMS Tempest. © Illustrated London News/Mary Evans Picture Library

aflame, the maiden voyage was over. Lasting seven hours thirty-three minutes, covering 248 miles, it was 15 times shorter than that of *Titanic*.

The dawn of 5th October revealed the smoking skeleton sprawled across the hillside. As the survivors were tended to, French authorities surveyed the scene while British investigators were flown in. Such was the faith of the Press in *R101's* capabilities, that only The *Express* newspaper ran the story that day. After a procession through Beauvais with military cortege, the victims were repatriated on 10th October via HMS *Tempest* and special trains. Laid in state in Westminster Hall, nearly 90,000 people visited to pay their respects during this period of national mourning. On 11th October, after a memorial service at St Paul's Cathedral, the coffins were escorted to Euston Station in a state procession including a guard of honour, the Cabinet and representatives from the Dominions, before being transported to Bedford by train. Walked the final 2 miles to Cardington, they were interred in a mass grave by the church, in sight of the sheds where they had departed. Present at this final service was Dr Eckener on behalf of the Zeppelin Company. In 1931 a memorial tomb was built, as were memorials near and on the crash site unveiled in 1933. A plaque commemorating the lying-in-state was laid in Westminster in November 2014.

Amazingly, despite the inferno *R101's* RAF pennant was found the next day still flying from her stern. Recovered, it now stands as a memorial in Cardington church.

An Inquiry was held, chaired by politician Sir John Simon, lasting from 28th October 1930 to 27th March 1931. All the technical witnesses supported the airworthiness of the airship, emphasising that she flew for several hours before suddenly

Memorial tomb to the R101 victims, Cardington. Author

being overwhelmed, but the Inquiry must have been hampered not only by the limited number of survivors but that many of the most relevant experts were lost in the disaster.

There would be, however, one unexpected piece of late testimony. In 1939 Eileen Garrett made headlines by presenting a detailed account of the crash. It made waves because the information was passed to her by the spirit of Flight Lieutenant Irwin during a séance. While the Air Ministry kept quiet, various investigators went through the account, all deciding the content was either common knowledge or nonsense and that Garrett was a fraud.

With the loss of *R101* Britain had not only lost many of its top airship experts and supporters, but the country had also lost faith in airship travel itself. As a letter by Harold Roxbee Cox, a Cardington engineer who did not fly, read:

'It is, I am afraid, the end of airships in this country'.

The scheme was immediately scrapped; the planned *R102-4* never materialised. The mooring mast at Cardington was demolished in 1941, while that at Karachi was never used by any airship.

R101 did not remain long in a French field. Thomas Ward & Sons were contracted to scrap her, much being turned into pots, pans and commemorative ashtrays. *R100*, having not flown since the disaster, was ignominiously broken up in November 1931, for the measly sum of £427. Originally intended to cost £1,200,000, the final total of the scheme was £2,396,948 and 48 lives.

Out of all the problems found, what had actually caused the disaster? Nothing conclusive could be proven, and all contributed to some degree, but according to the Inquiry it is believed to have been something like this:

By 2:00am, *R101* had been buffeted by storms for hours, soaking her cover. As she got heavier through both this and leaks, she became increasingly

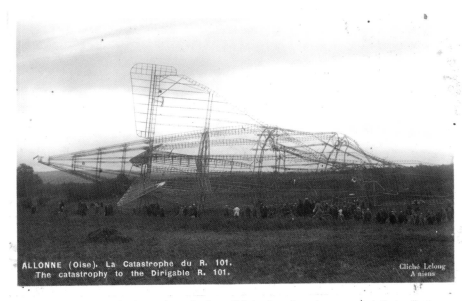

Period postcard of the skeletal stern (note the flag still flying from the extreme rear). *Author's collection*

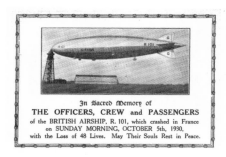

3n Sacred Memory of
THE OFFICERS, CREW and PASSENGERS
of the BRITISH AIRSHIP, R. 101, which crashed in France
on SUNDAY MORNING, OCTOBER 5th, 1930,
with the Loss of 48 Lives. May Their Souls Rest in Peace.

An 'In Memoriam' card commemorating the disaster. *Author's collection*

dependent on forward motion to give dynamic lift. But this placed increasing aerodynamic force on her bow – an area where the faulty cover had not been replaced. At 2:06am it began to fail in the wind, forcing her nose downwards through drag, before tearing completely, triggering her first dive at 2:07am. Hunt pulled up the elevators, bringing her level, but the dive coupled with the storm on the exposed gasbags fatally weakened them and they split. Plainly realising they had a terminal problem Steff slowed the engines. Less experienced than his colleagues, this action reduced dynamic lift and the bow, essentially without buoyant hydrogen, fell into the second dive. The cause of the fire remains unknown – the Inquiry suggesting electrical wiring – but with hot and damaged diesels crushed into her hull, her faulty engines may have been her final undoing. The true cause will never been known for certain, but with this calamity Britain was out of the airship age.

Along with technical reasons, there were other broader factors. Quoting the Inquiry:

'In the construction of the R101 the designers broke away almost completely from conventional methods...originality and courage in design are not to be depreciated, but there is an obvious danger in giving too many separate hostages to fortune at one time.'

Most significant though was their comment:

'The R101 started for India before she could be regarded as having emerged successfully from all the exhaustive steps proper to the experimental stage.'

This shows the overriding factor – with time, issues could have been fixed. But instead the project was increasingly rushed to meet the Imperial Conference. While much of this was due to Thomson, it was more enthusiasm than direct interference on his part and he was not aware of the full situation. Dowding had been concerned lest Thomson exert pressure but found this unwarranted – Thomson saying on 2nd October to both him and Colmore:

'You mustn't allow my natural impatience or anxiety to start to influence you in any way. You must use your considered judgment.'

But those high up within the Royal Airship Works were equally impatient and felt they had much to prove; this was a Government-funded project after all. Although not Thomson's fault alone, and despite his claims, political reasoning overtook engineering practice. To quote the Inquiry:

> *'It is impossible to avoid the conclusion that the R101 would not have started for India on the evening of 4th October if it had not been that reasons of public policy were considered as making it highly desirable for her to do so if she could.'*

Later working with record breaker Donald Campbell, survivor Harry Leech declared: 'One thing the *R101* proved is that politics and experimental work don't mix.'

But contrary to general claims and gross oversimplification *R101* had some good features, *R100* some bad. Neither ship was in any way perfect nor commercially practical – the only real reason *R100* is seen as superior today is through the fame of her designers and for having not crashed. However, while the project cost Britain some of her leading aeronautical experts, Dr Eckener emphasised the importance of what had been achieved, stating of the knowledge gained (notably construction and mooring techniques) that 'airship travel could not be developed without it'.

With the loss of *R101* the Imperial Airship Scheme came to an end. But circumstances would mean that *R101* would fly again. Approximately five tons of wrecked duralumin was purchased by the Zeppelin Company and is believed by some as used in Dr Eckener's newest airship – bigger, better, safer:

Hindenburg…

Spectators gathering to view the remains of R101.
© Illustrated London News/*Mary Evans Picture Library*

SELECT BIBLIOGRAPHY

If you have found these events of interest and wish to learn more, here is the next step:

The Olympic Class
R. Ballard, *The Discovery of the Titanic*, Warner Books (1995).
L. Beesley, *The Loss of the SS. Titanic: Its Stories and its Lessons*, Houghton Mifflin Co (1912).
J. Eaton & C. Haas, *Titanic: Triumph and Tragedy*, W.W. Norton & Co (1995).
S. Halpern et al., *Report into the SS Titanic: A Centennial Reappraisal*, The History Press (2011).
S. Mills, *The Unseen Britannic*, The History Press (2014).
P. Mylon, *The Unseen Olympic*, The History Press (2013).

Quintinshill
J.A.B. Hamilton, *Britain's Greatest Rail Disaster: The Quintinshill Blaze of 1915*, Allen & Unwin (1969).
J. Richards & A. Searle, *The Quintinshill Conspiracy: The Shocking True Story Behind Britain's Worst Rail Disaster*, Pen & Sword Books (2013).
G. Routledge, *The Sorrows of Quintinshill*, Arthuret Publishers (2002).
J. Thomas, *Gretna: Britain's Worst Railway Disaster (1915)*, David & Charles (1969).

Lusitania
R. Ballard & S. Dunmore, *Exploring the Lusitania*, Weidenfeld & Nicolson (1995).
C. Lauriat, *The Lusitania's Last Voyage*, Houghton Mifflin & Co (1915).
D. Preston, *Wilful Murder: The Sinking Of The Lusitania*, Doubleday (2015).
E. Sauder, *The Unseen Lusitania: The Ship in Rare Illustrations*, The History Press (2015).

The Tay Bridge
J. Prebble, *The High Girders: Tay Bridge Disaster, 1879*, Macmillan (1968).
L.T.C. Rolt, *Red for Danger*, David & Charles (1976).
J. Thomas, *Tay Bridge Disaster: New Light on the 1879 Tragedy*, David & Charles (1972).

Princess Alice
J. Lock, *The Princess Alice Disaster*, Robert Hale Ltd (2013).
W. Neal, *With Disastrous Consequences: London Disasters, 1830-1917*, Hisarlik Press (1992).
G. Thurston, *The Great Thames Disaster*, Allen & Unwin (1965).

The British Imperial Airship Scheme
T. Coates, *R101: The Airship Disaster, 1930 (Uncovered Editions)*, The Stationary Office (1999).
J. Leasor, *The Millionth Chance: the Story of R.101*, H. Hamilton (1957).
N. Walmsley, *R101: A Pictorial History*, The History Press (2010).